How to Draw Zoo Animals (Step by step instructions on how to draw cartoon zoo animals)

This book has over 300 detailed illustrations that demonstrate how to easily draw 36 cartoon zoo animals step by step

J.P. Manning

1. The use of ellipses in grids can be very helpful when you want to create round shapes.

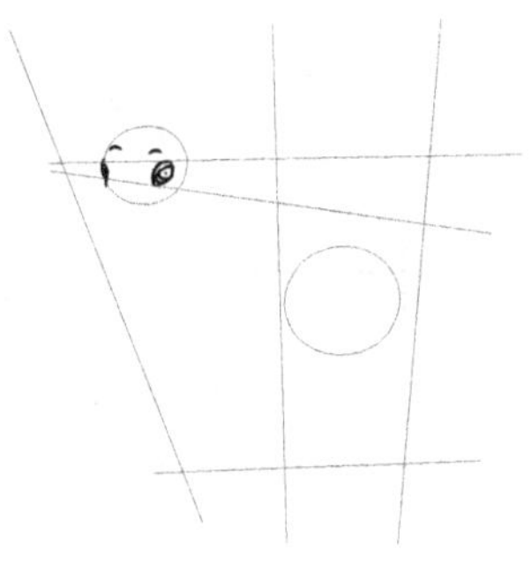

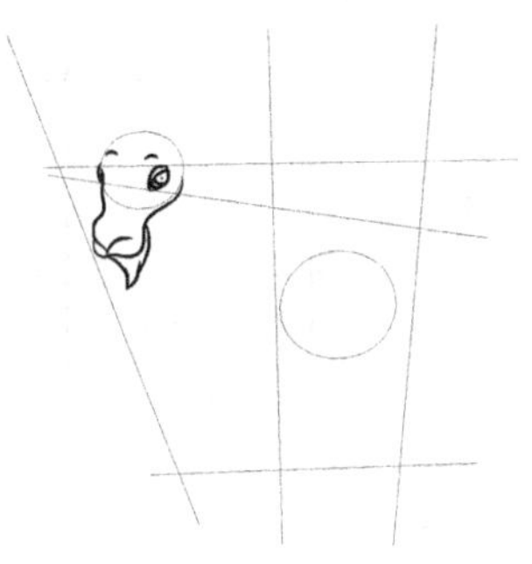

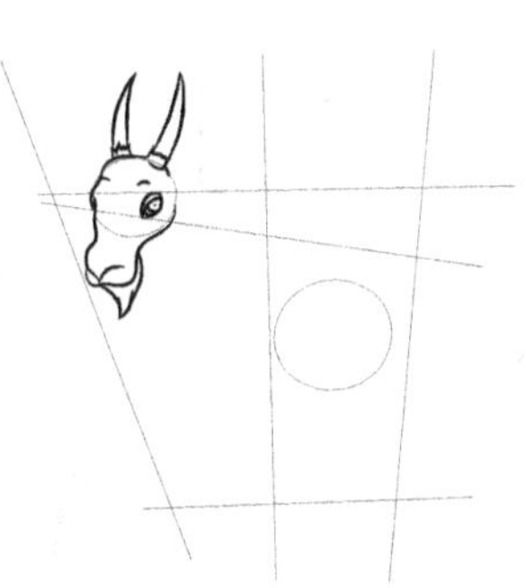

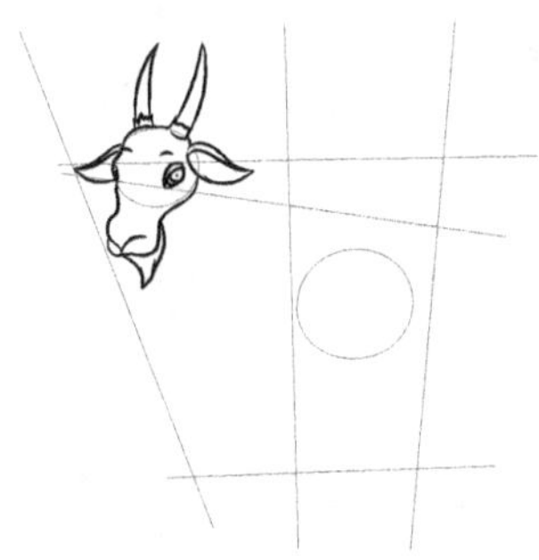

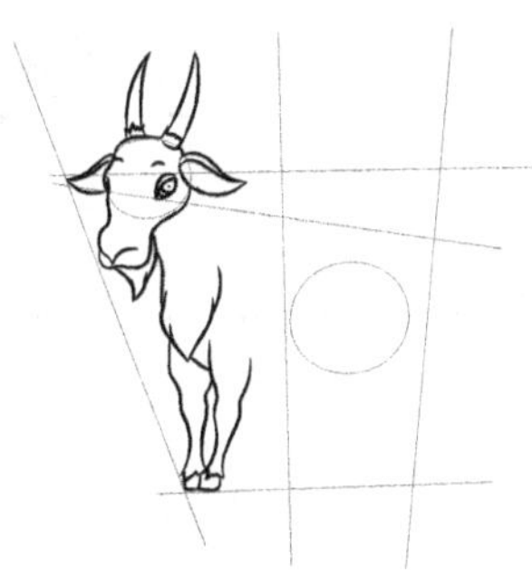

Goats, domesticated early, are agile, intelligent, and social. Known for climbing, they have wide vision from rectangular pupils and communicate through bleats. As browsers, they prefer leaves and twigs. Diverse breeds and easily digestible milk underscore their economic and historical significance.

2. Drawing lines on your grid will help you to draw eyes that are focused on a distant object.

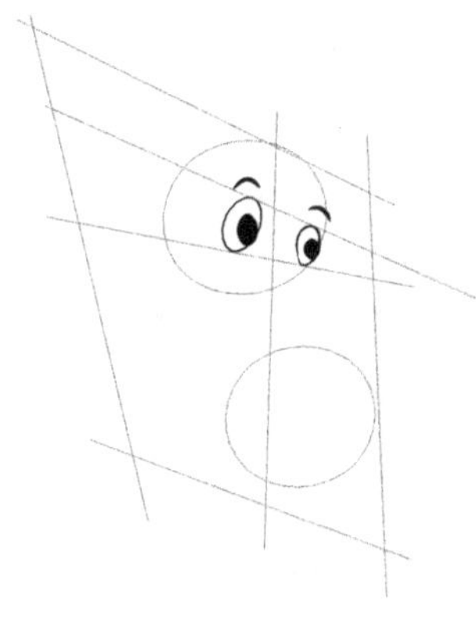
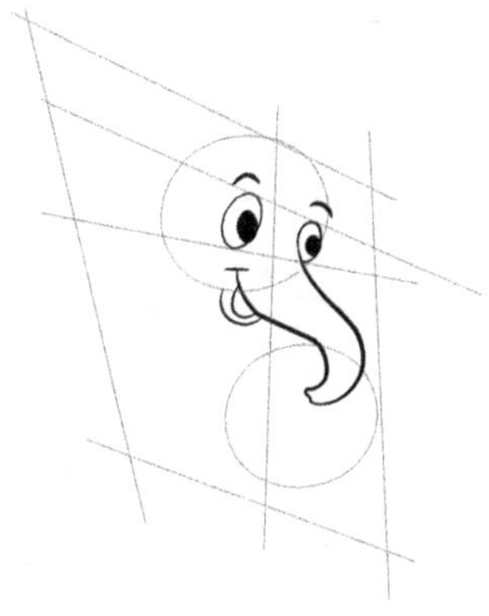

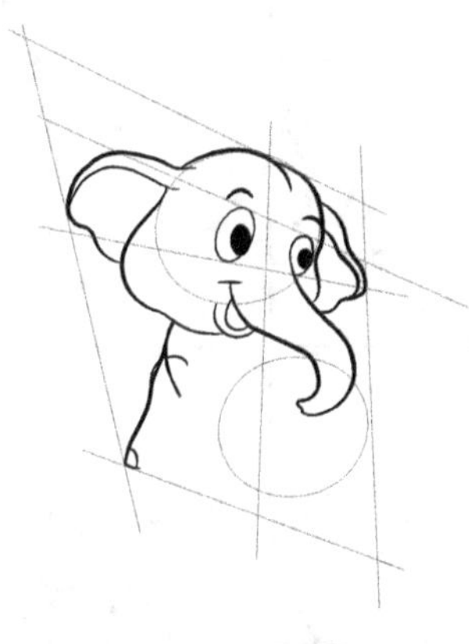
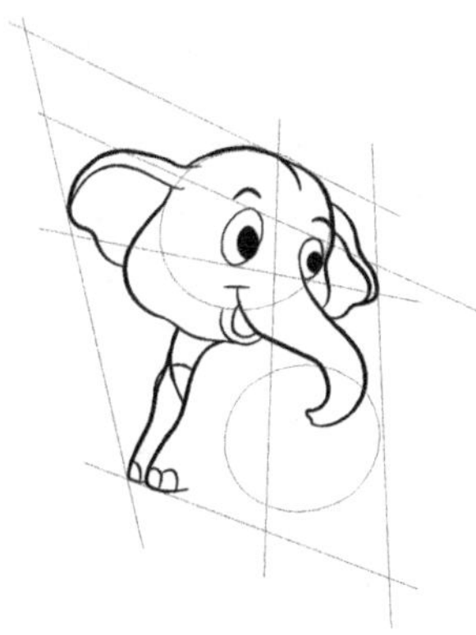

Elephants, the largest land animals, have remarkable memories, complex social structures, and use their trunks for various tasks. They communicate through infrasound and vibrations, are essential for ecosystems, and show emotions like joy and grief.

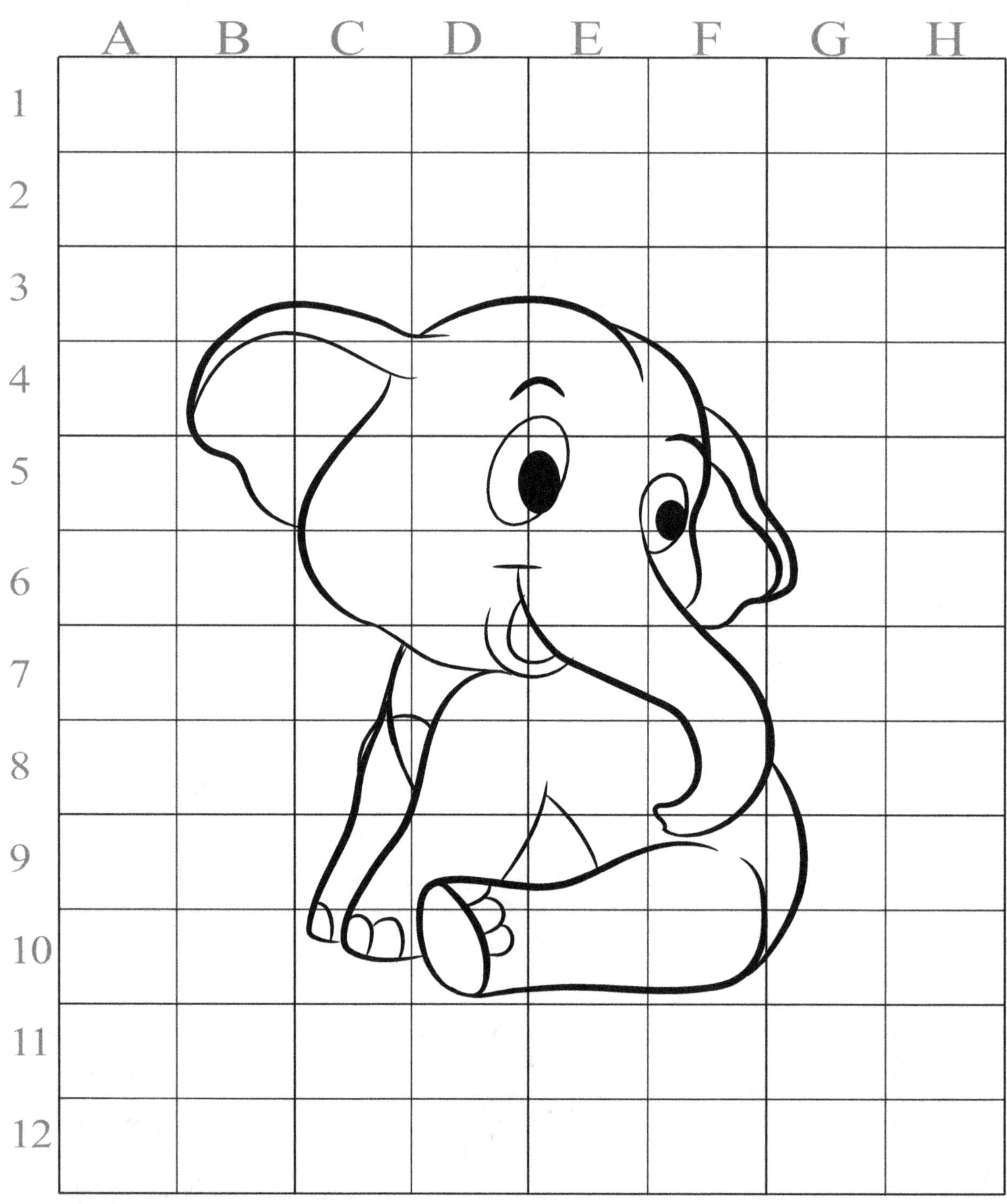

3. Start your drawing with the eyes and
construct a face around it next.

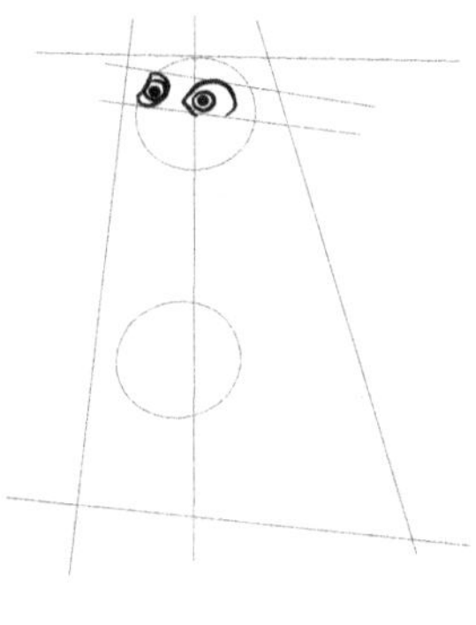

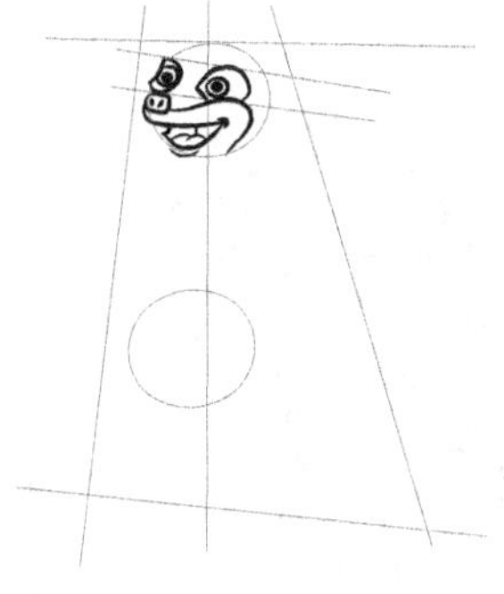

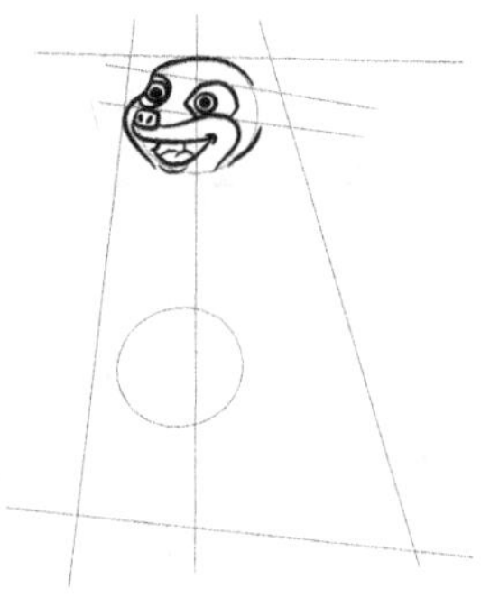

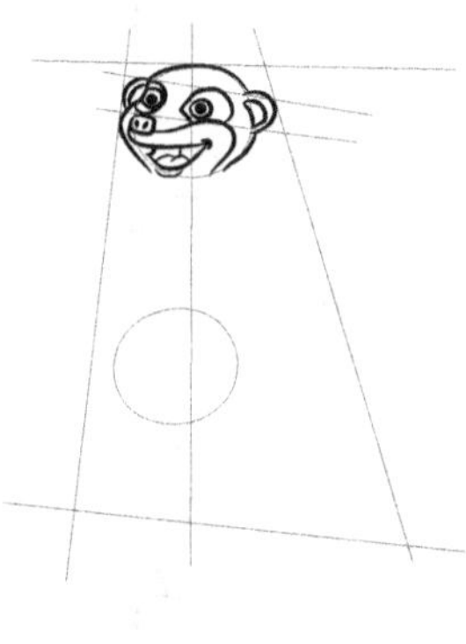

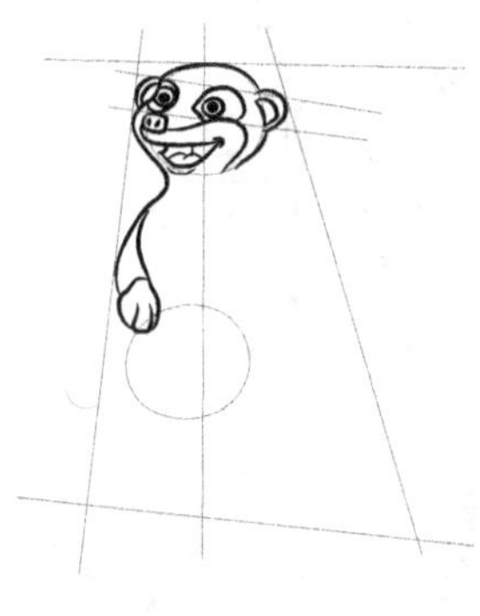

Meerkats live in social mobs, use sentinels for predator watch, and communicate with varied vocalizations. They stand on two legs to survey their surroundings and have cooperative behaviors, including communal care for pups.

4. Draw the head first and then build the rest of the body around it.

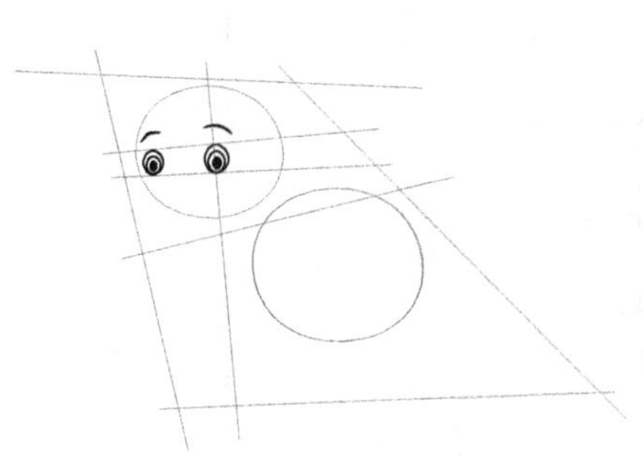

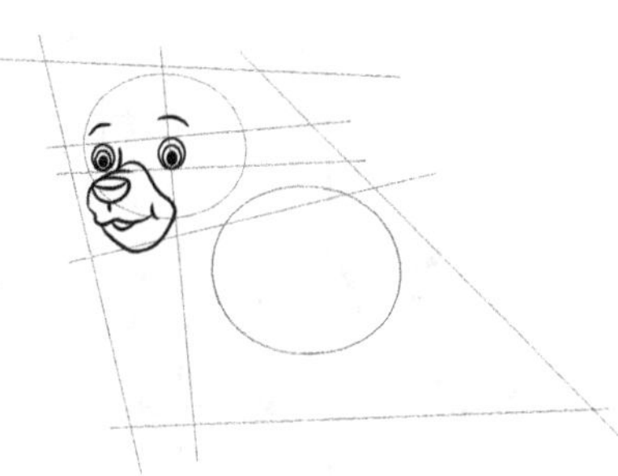

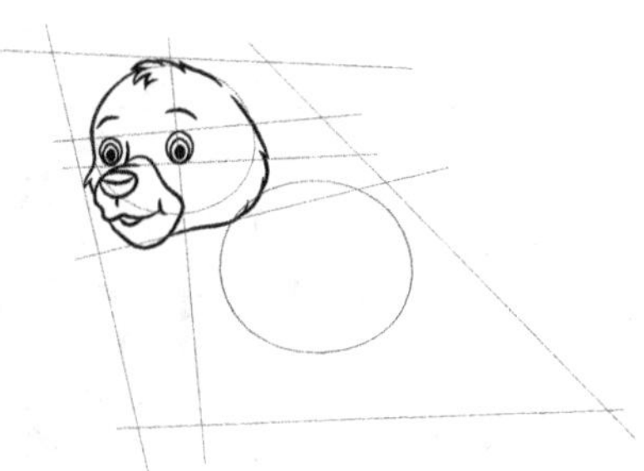

Bears are intelligent, with excellent memories and complex behaviors. They can stand on two legs, communicate through vocalizations and body language, and have a keen sense of smell. Varied diets range from berries to fish. Some species, like the polar bear, are skilled swimmers

5. Separate your grid into sections to help you decide how you want to proportion your drawing. This can help you to alter the height of your character.

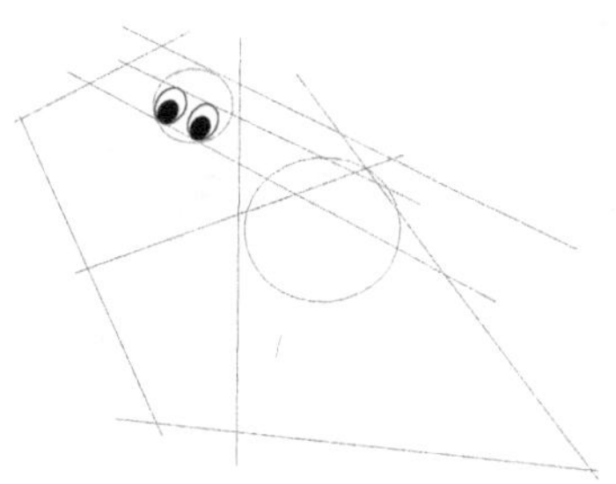

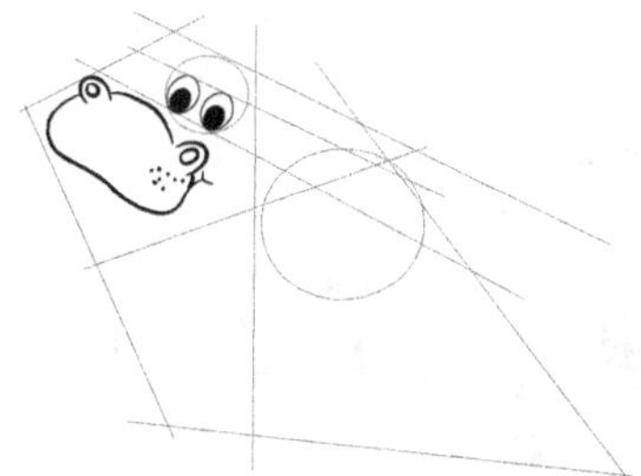

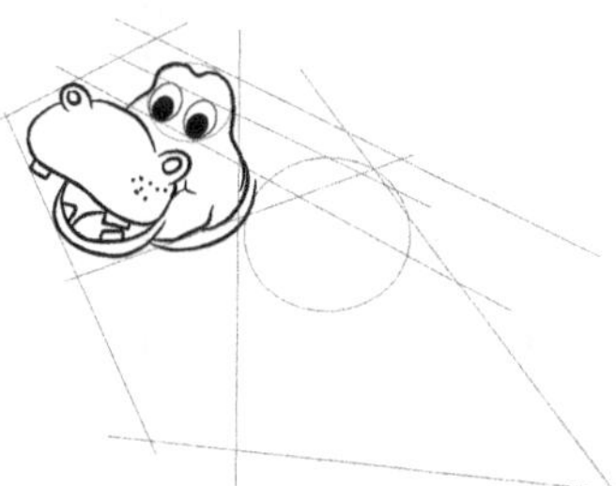

Hippos are large, semi-aquatic mammals that can run up to 19 mph. They spend most of their time in water to stay cool and communicate vocally. Vital for ecosystems, hippos create channels and pools. Surprisingly aggressive, they're among Africa's most dangerous animals.

6. A simple grid can often help to guide you when drawing. After you have drawn your grid, begin with the eyes.

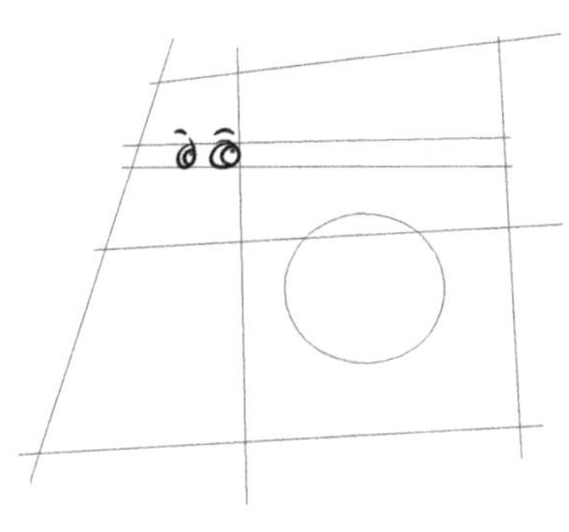 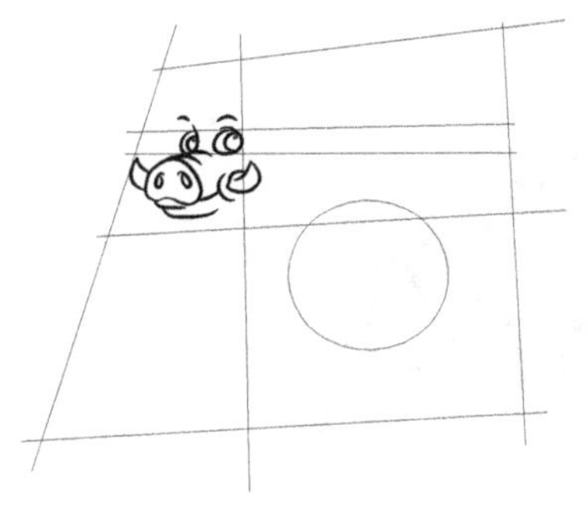 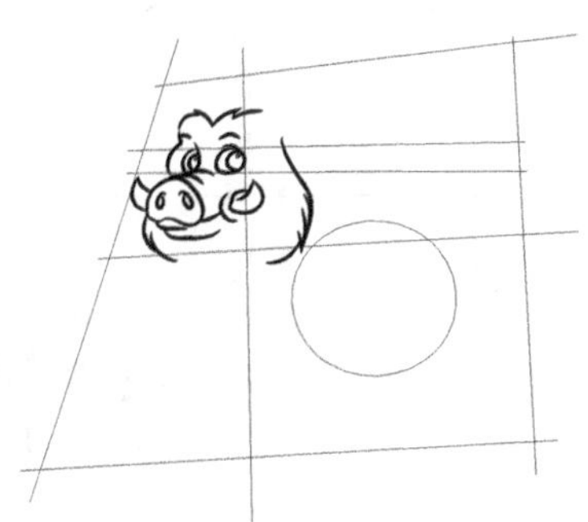

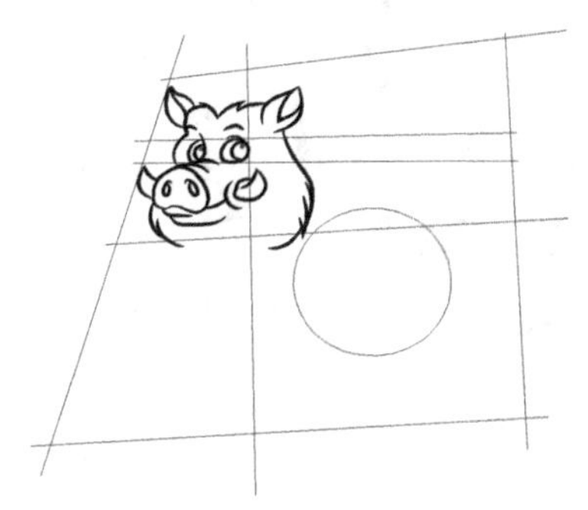 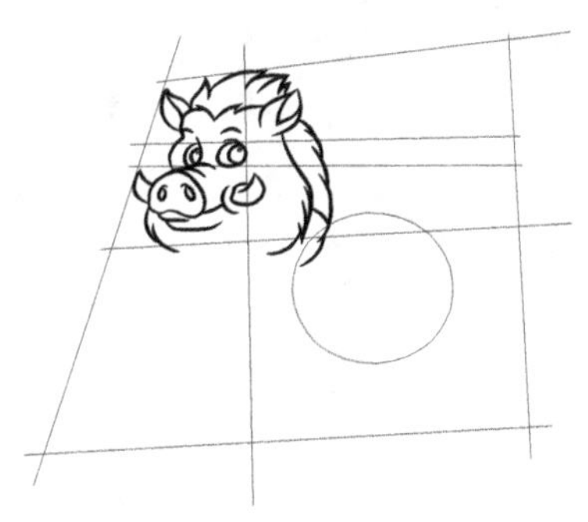 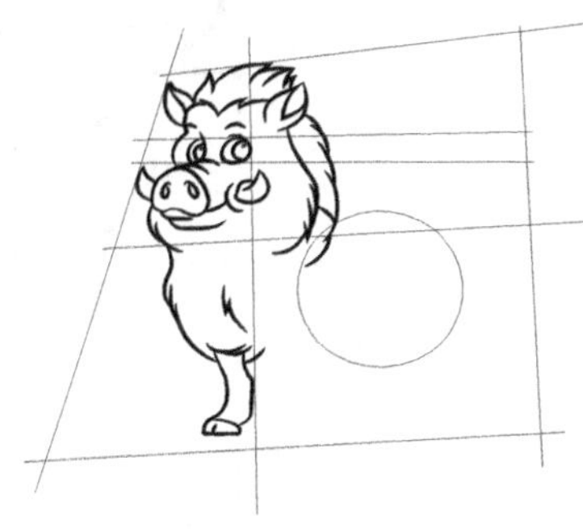

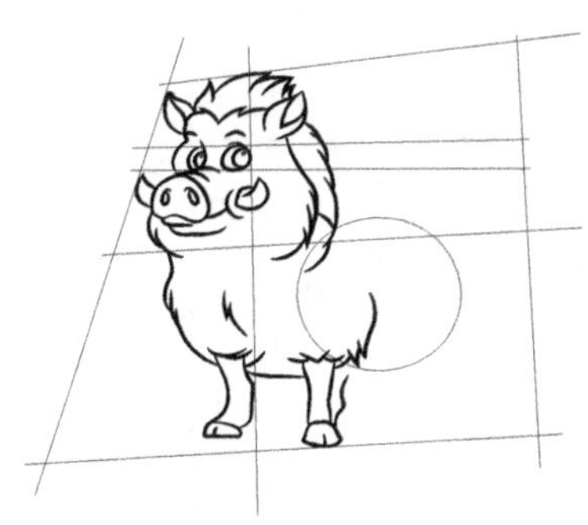  

A warthog is a wild pig species native to Africa. Known for their distinctive appearance, including large tusks and facial warts, they primarily inhabit savannas and grasslands. Warthogs are omnivorous and use their tusks for defense against predators and for digging roots and bulbs.

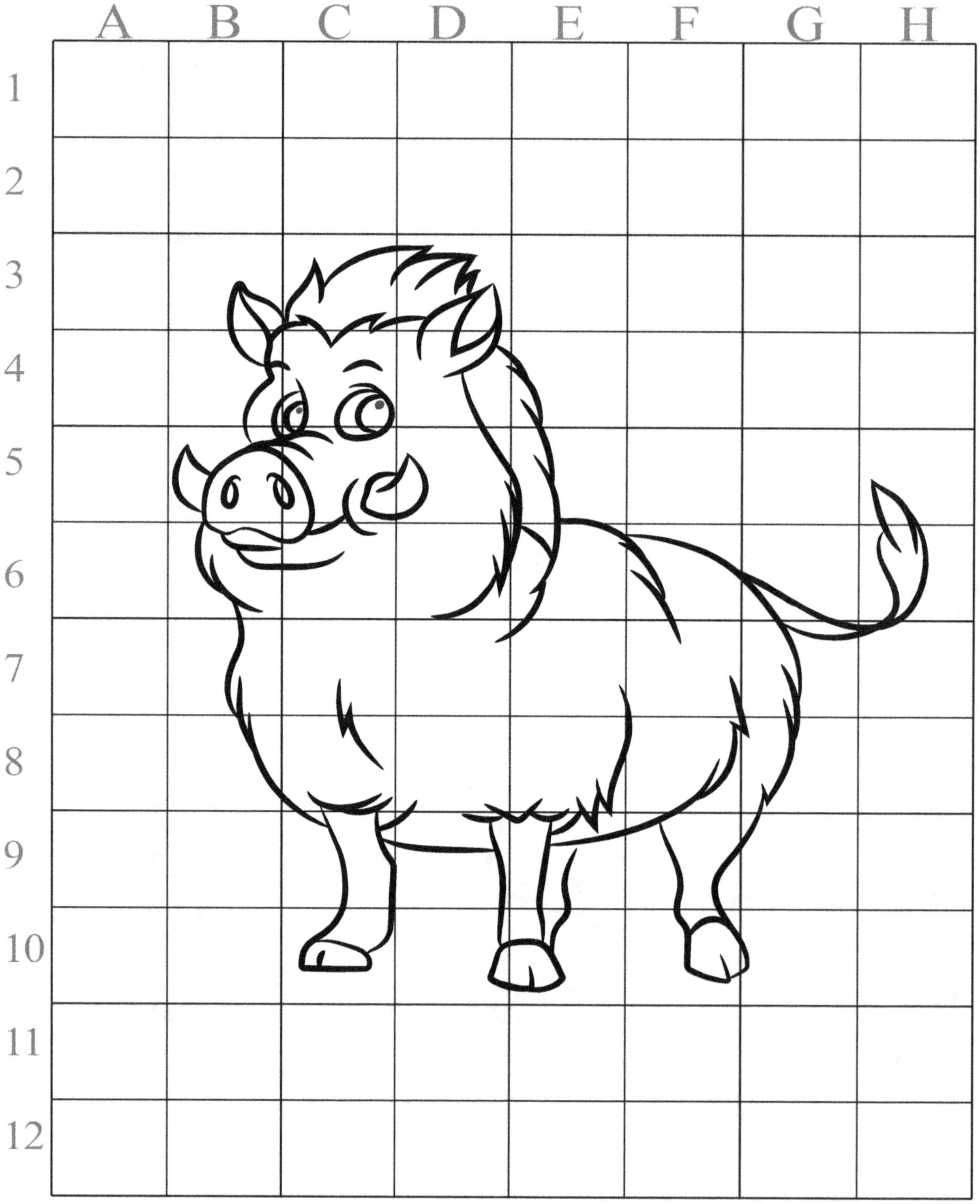

7. Try enlarging
different parts of
your drawings to
create different
effects.

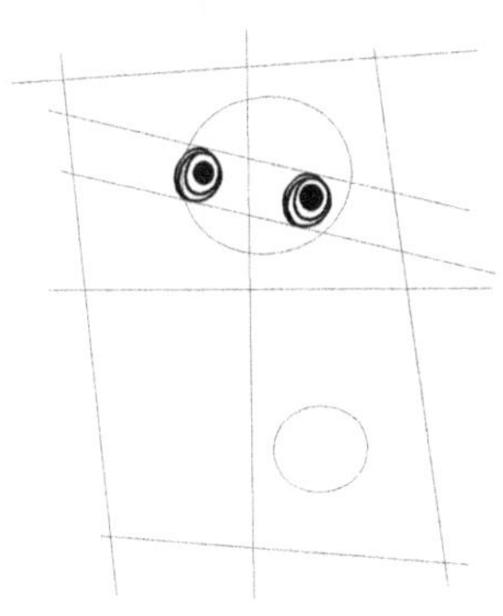 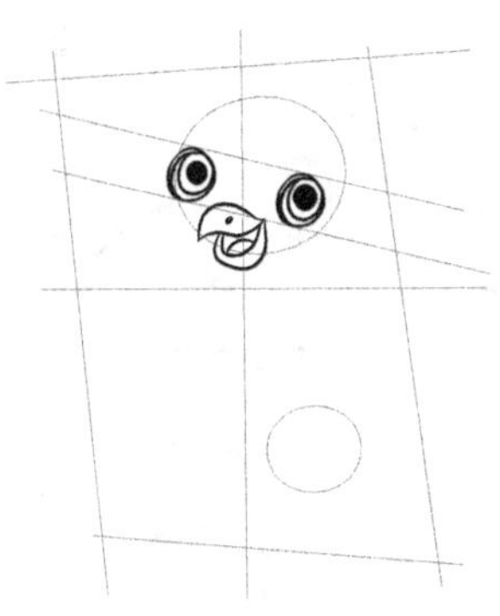 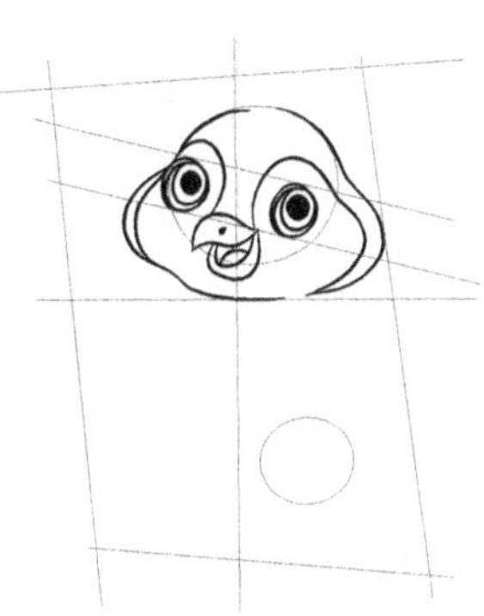

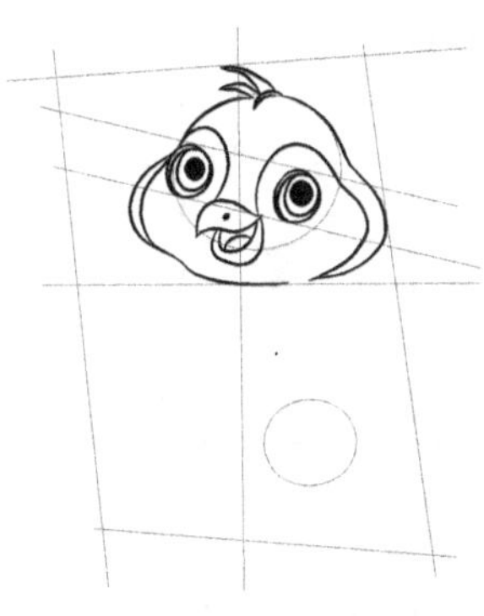  

Penguins are flightless birds found in the Southern Hemisphere. They swim gracefully using flipper-like wings for propulsion. They form large colonies for breeding and exhibit monogamous behavior. Penguins are adapted to cold climates, with thick waterproof feathers and a unique tuxedo-like appearance.

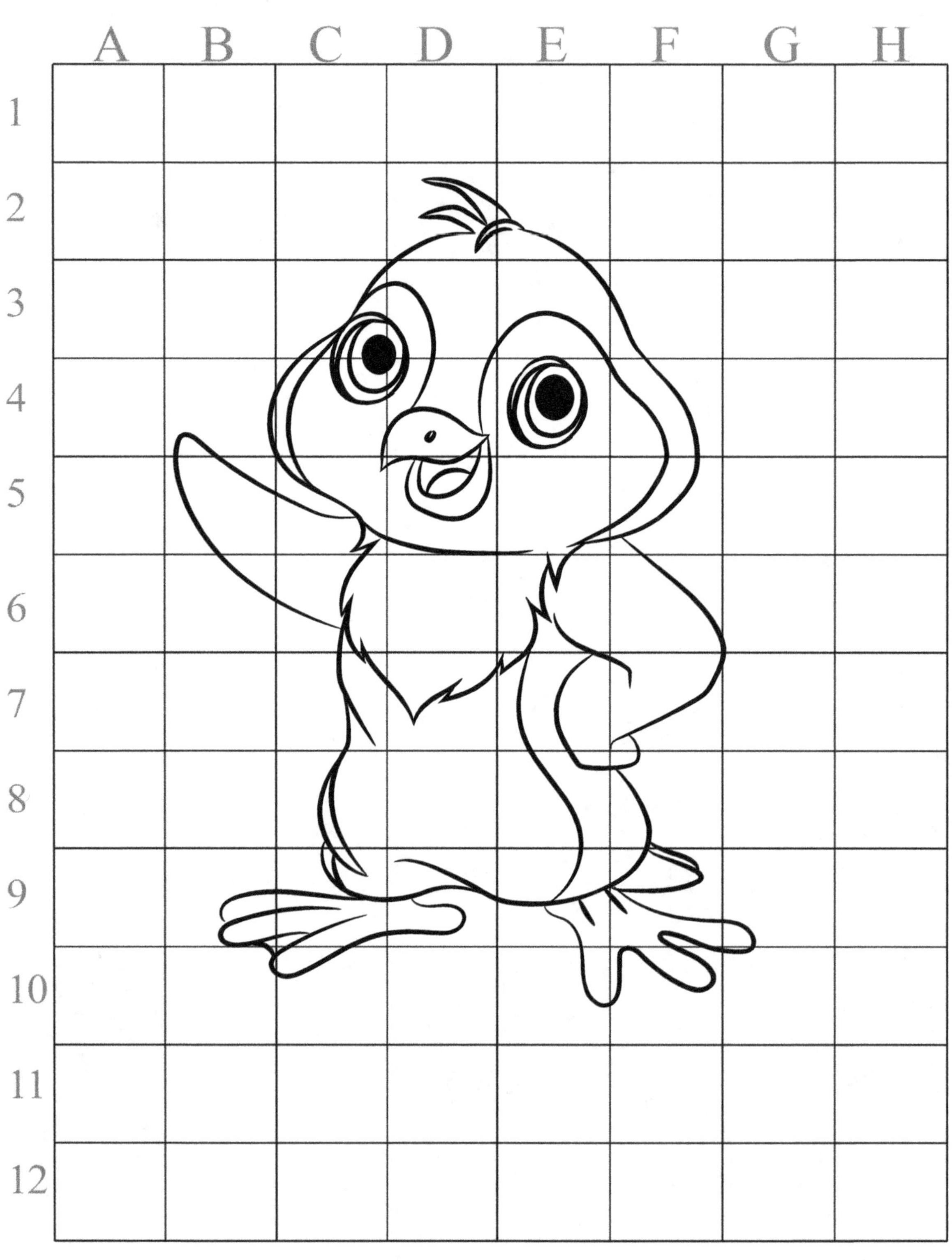

8. Triangles in your grid can be very helpful to create characters with more angular features.

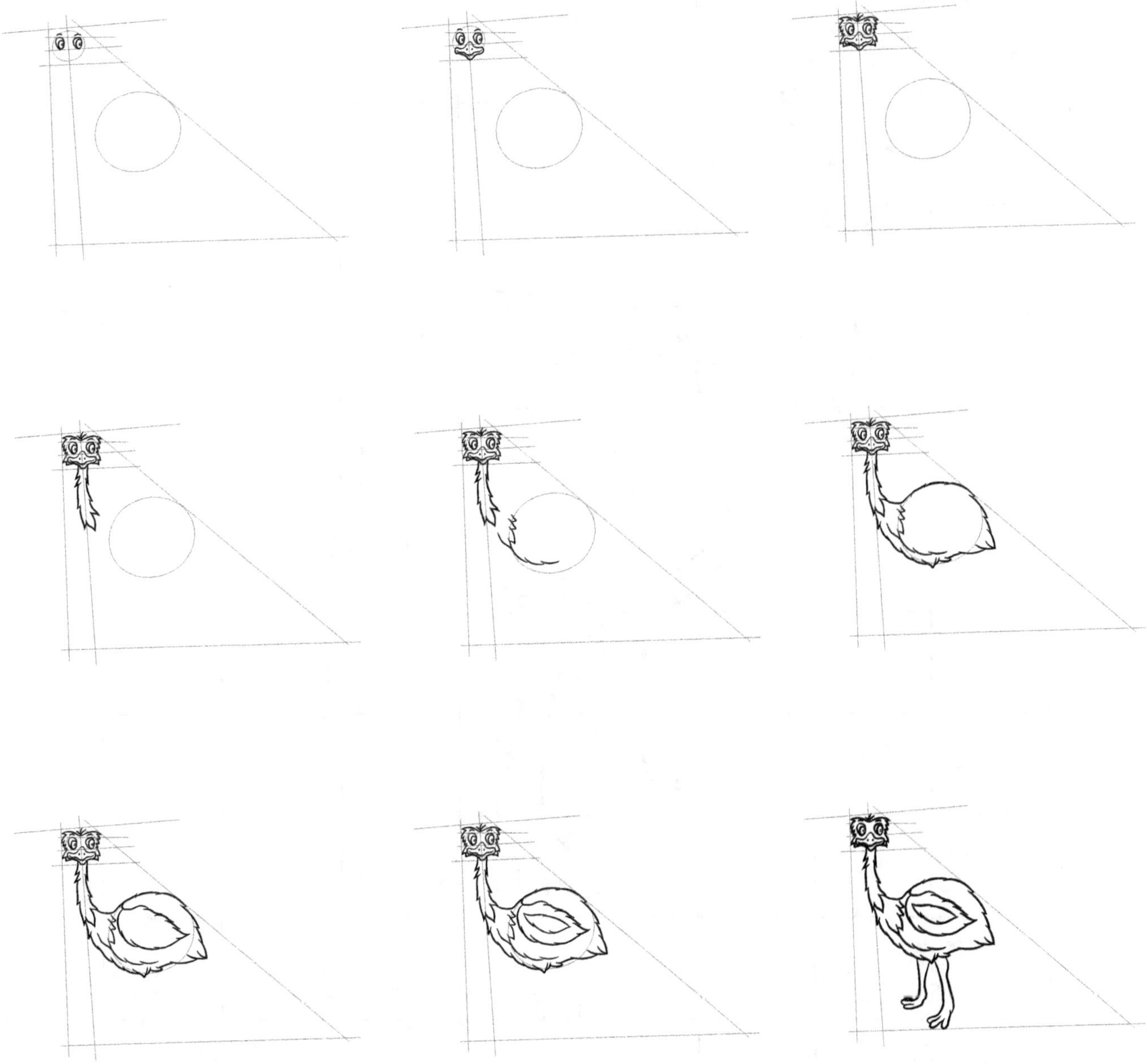

Emus are flightless birds native to Australia. They are the second-largest bird by height, with long legs adapted for speed. Emus are known for their distinctive drumming sound during mating season and play an important role in Australian indigenous culture.

9. After you have drawn your character's head it is easier to add small details.

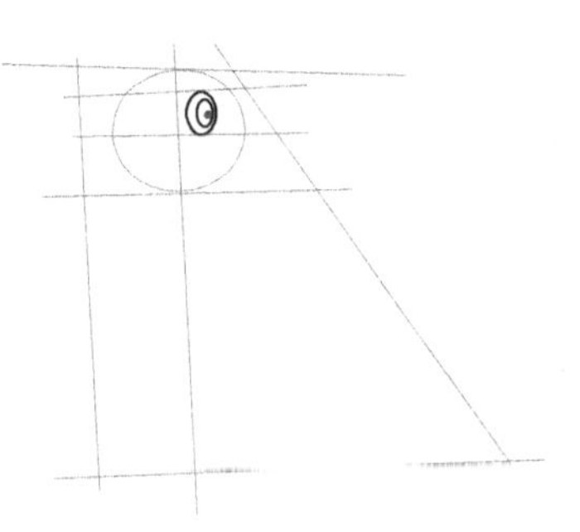

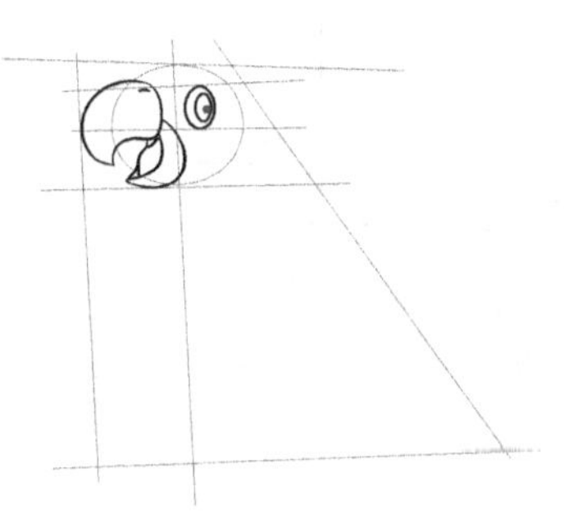

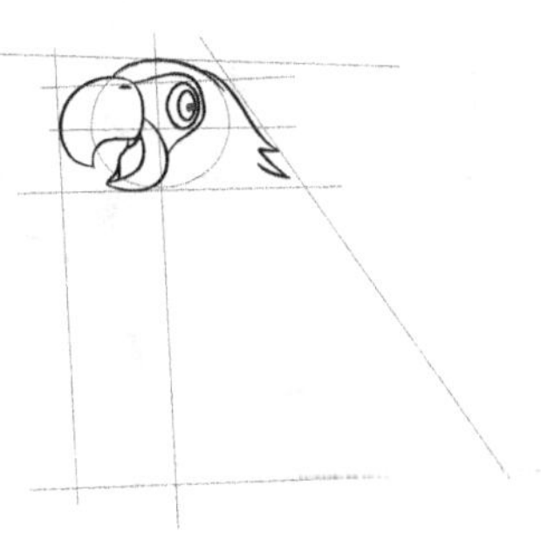

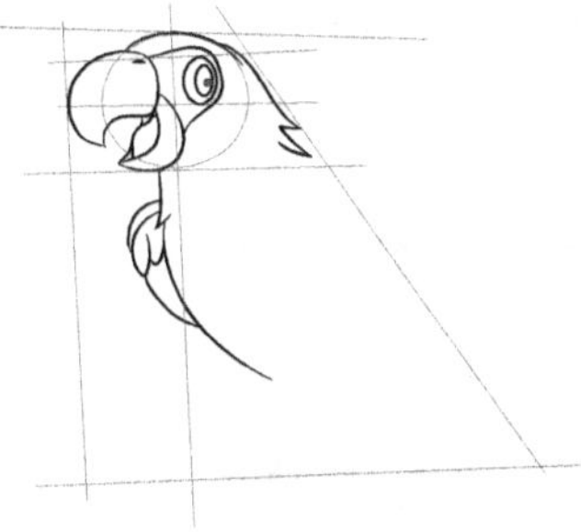

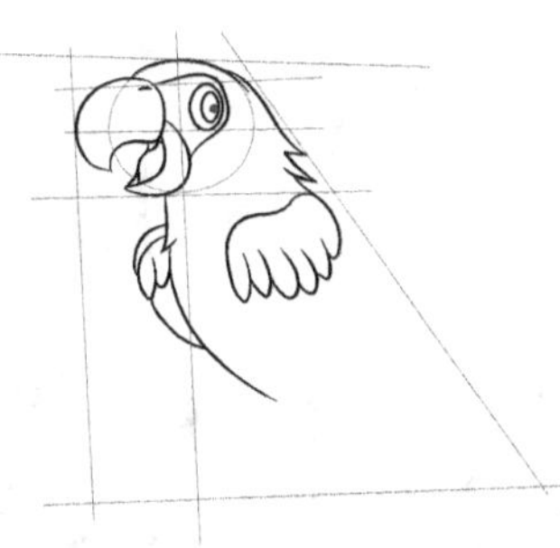

Parrots are intelligent birds with colorful plumage and the ability to mimic speech and sounds. They have zygodactyl feet for grasping objects, form strong bonds, and are found in various habitats worldwide. Known for their playfulness and problem-solving skills, they are popular pets and subjects of research.

10. Creating a caricature involves
exaggerating the features of your character.

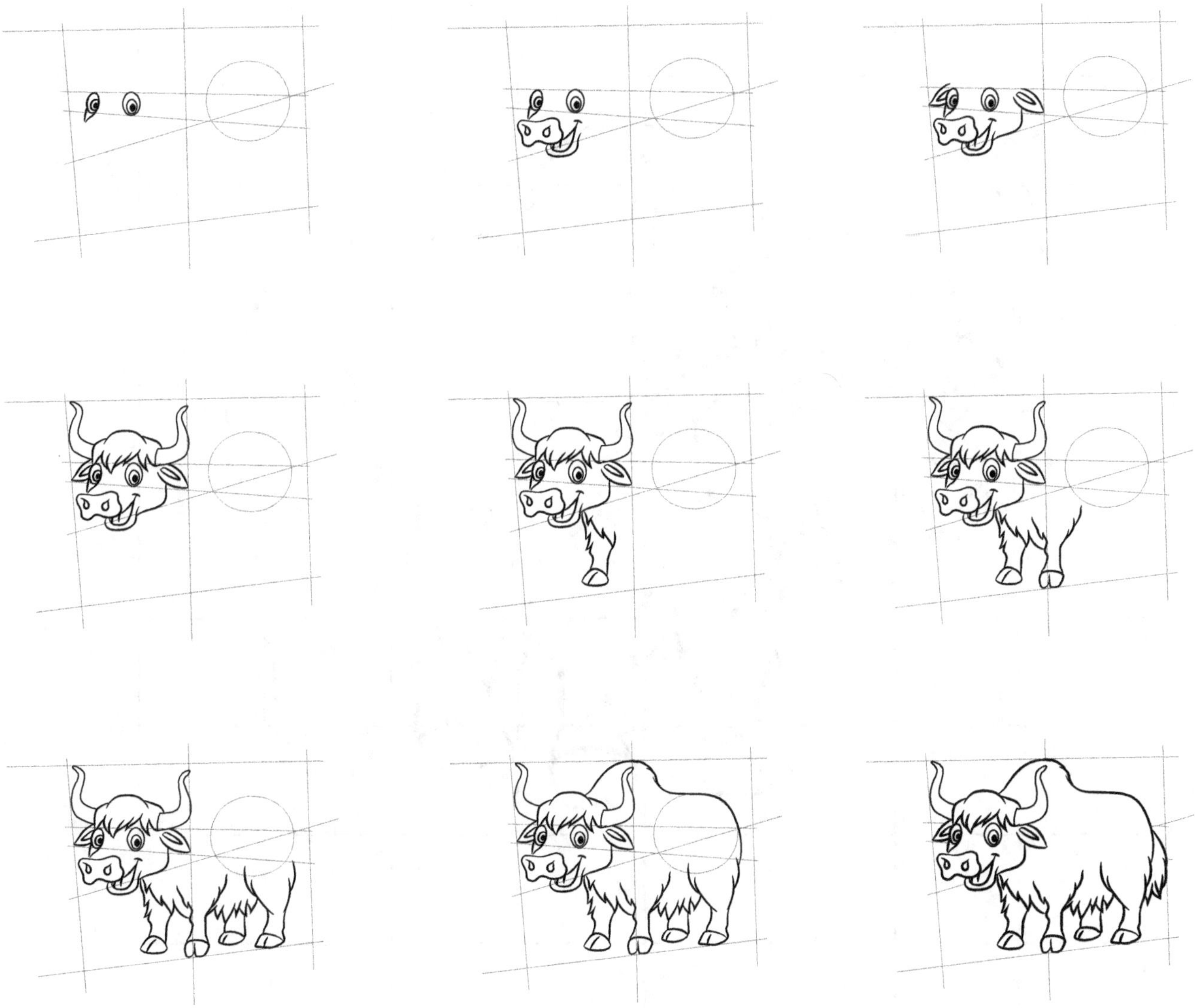

Buffalo, or bison in North America, are large herbivorous mammals known for their robust build and distinctive horns. They once roamed the Great Plains in vast herds, led by dominant females in matriarchal groups. They symbolize strength in indigenous cultures and play a crucial role in grassland ecosystems.

11. You can turn
your character's
head while keeping
the position of its
body the same.

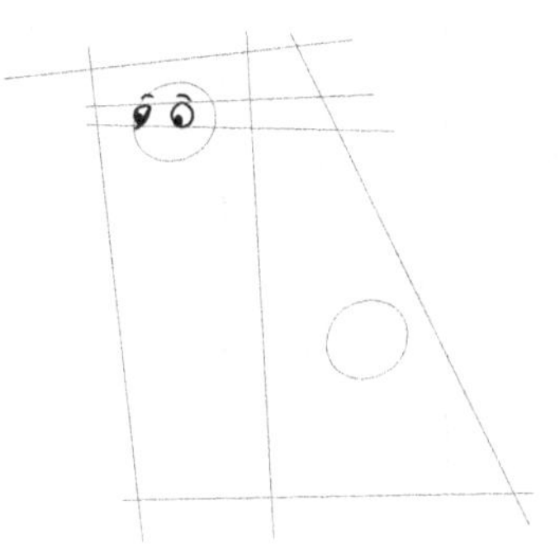

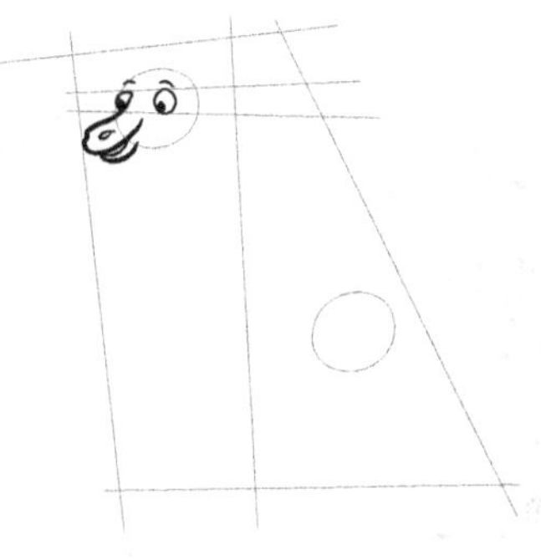

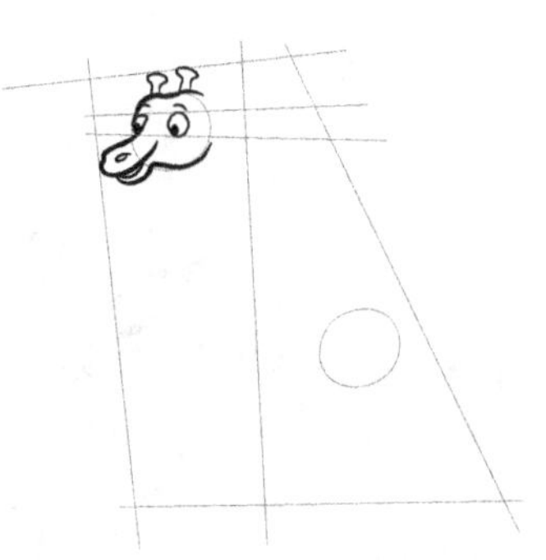

Giraffes are the world's tallest land animals, known for their long necks and distinctive coat patterns. They use their height to browse leaves from tall trees and communicate through infrasound. Giraffes are gentle herbivores found in savannas and grasslands across Africa.

12. When starting a more complex drawing it is best to think of it as a lot of small parts. Focusing on one small part at a time will make your project feel less overwhelming.

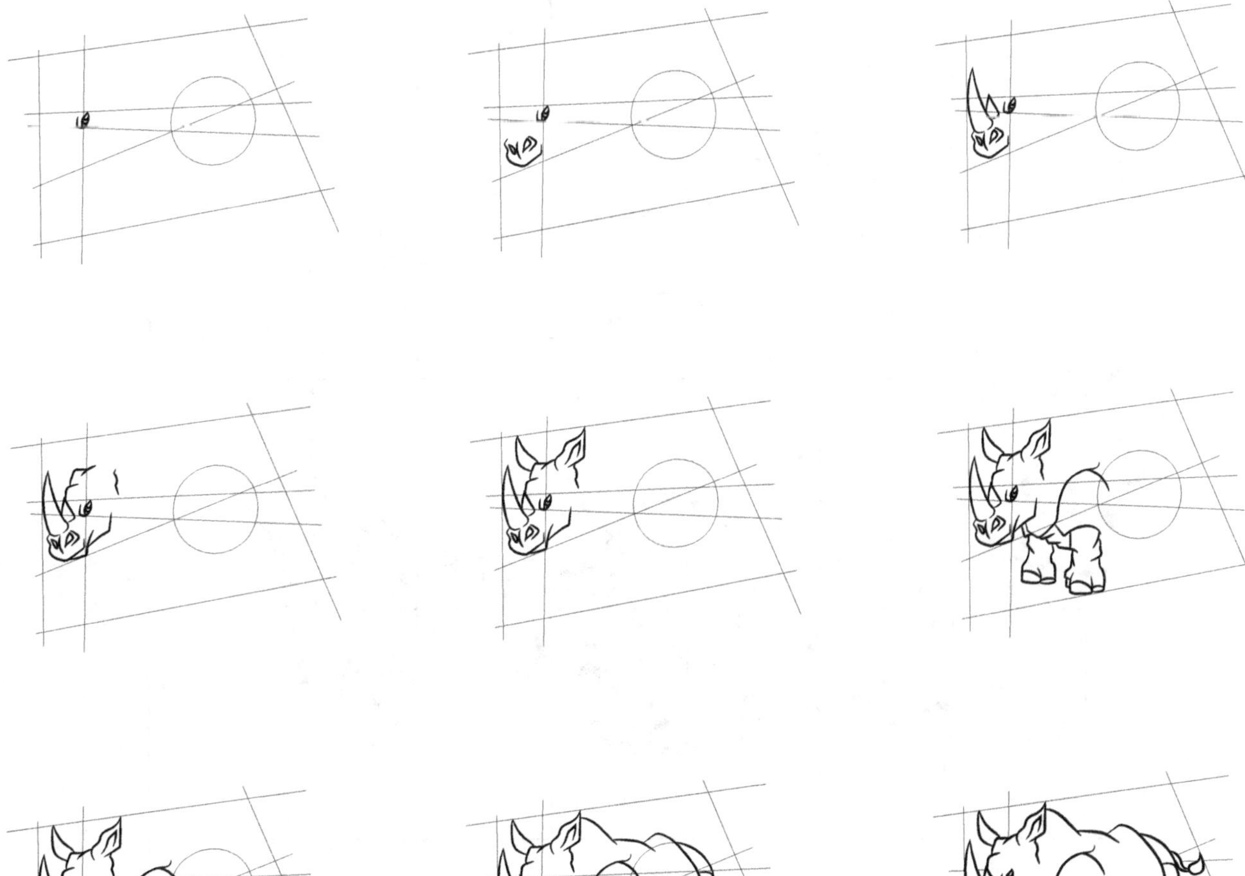

Rhinoceroses, or rhinos, are large herbivorous mammals with distinctive horns made of keratin. They are found in Africa and Asia and play crucial roles in their ecosystems. Despite their size, rhinos can run up to 35 mph. They are critically endangered due to poaching for their horns.

13. Changing the
position of your
characters eyebrows
can slightly alter
emotional expression.

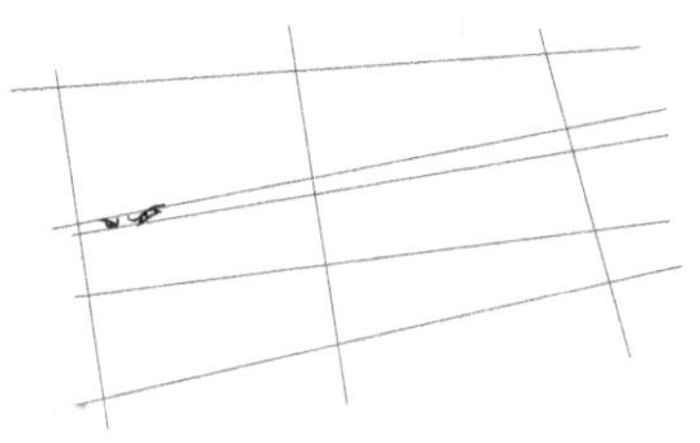
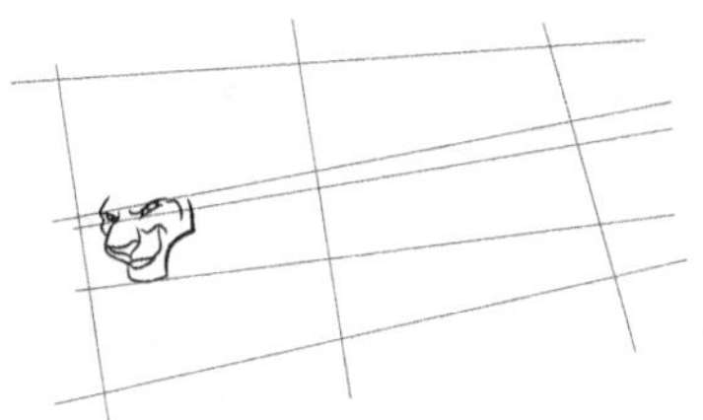
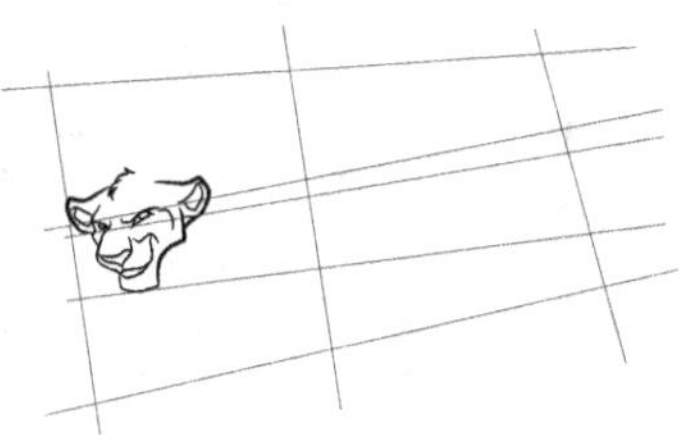

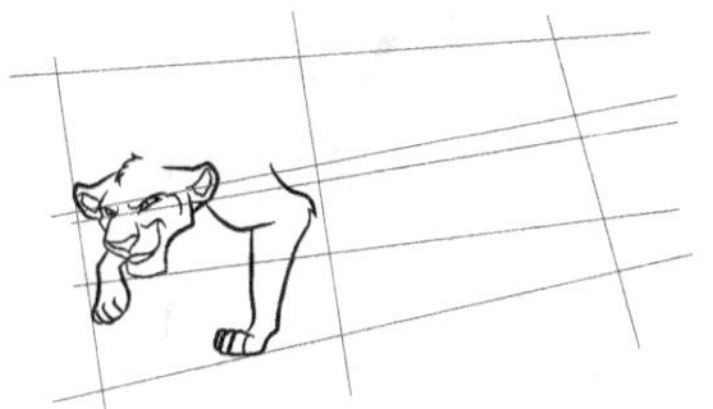
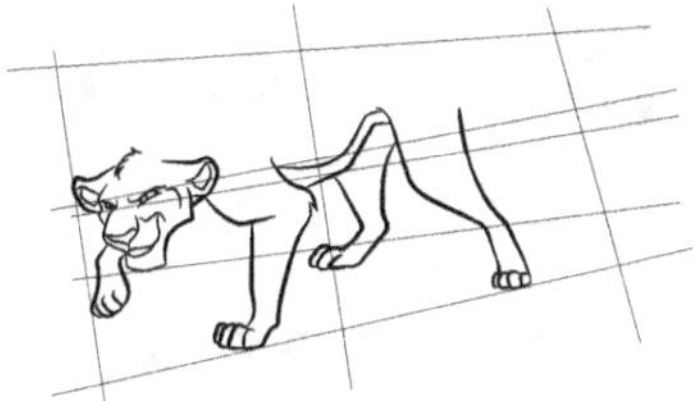
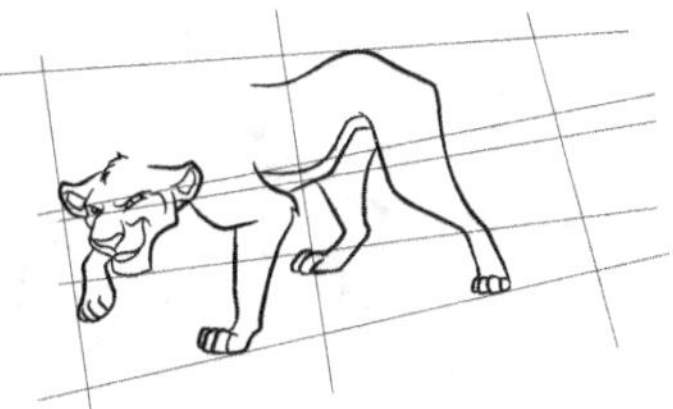

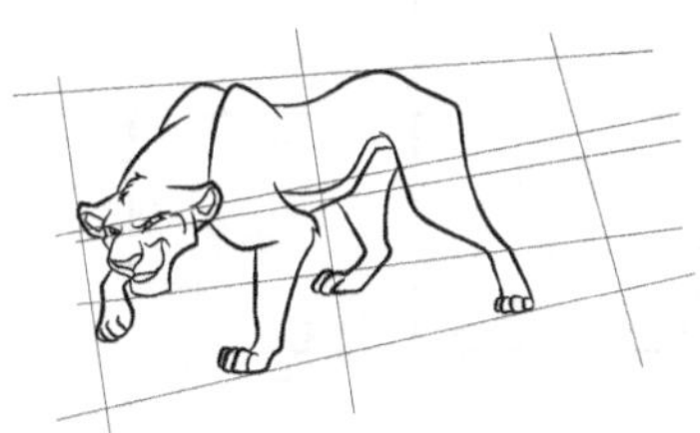
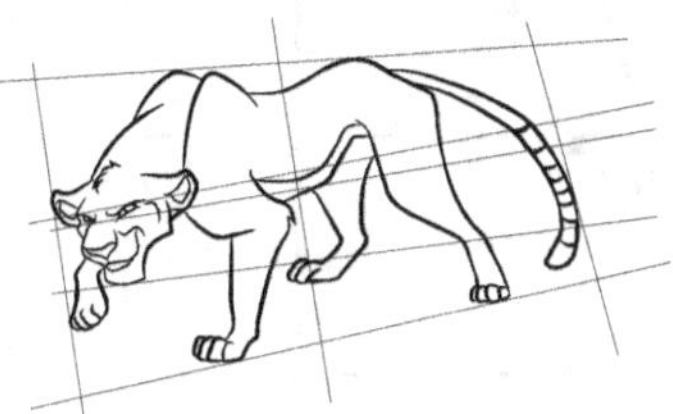
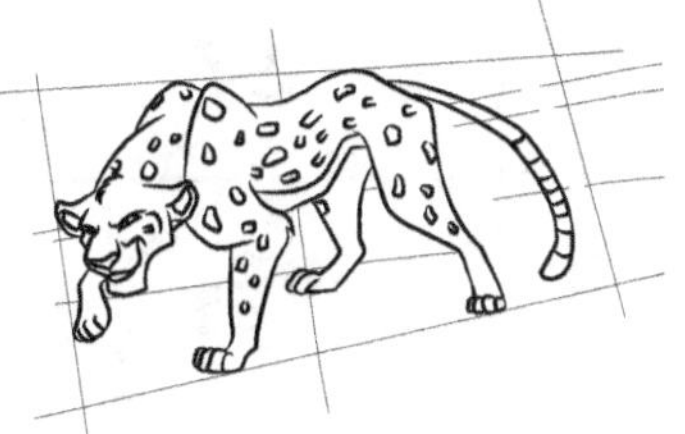

Leopards are agile big cats found across Africa and parts of Asia, known for their spotted coat that provides excellent camouflage. They are versatile hunters, capable of climbing trees with prey and adapting to various habitats from dense forests to savannas. Leopards are solitary and elusive predators, vital to ecosystem balance.

14. Your character may have a basic shape that you can attempt to outline using your initial grid.

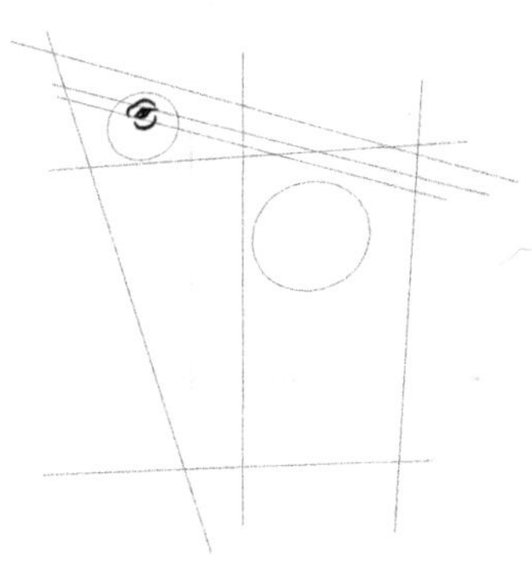
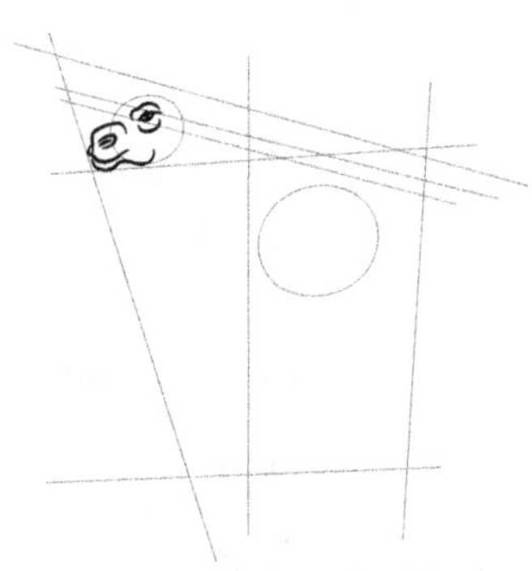
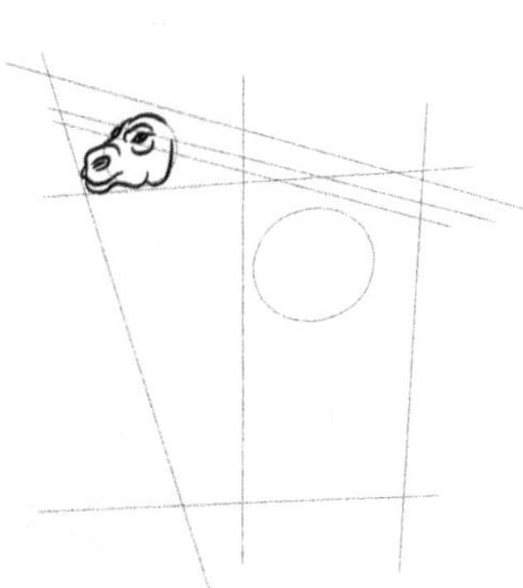

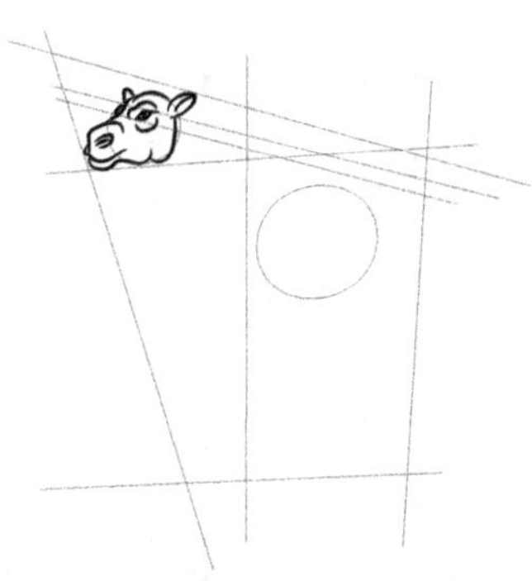
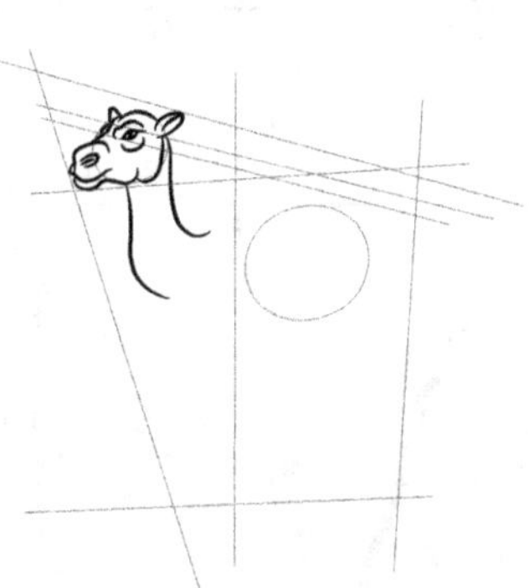

The one-humped camel, also known as the dromedary camel, is native to the Middle East and North Africa. It's well-adapted to desert environments, with a single hump storing fat for energy, enabling it to survive long periods without water. Dromedaries are used for transportation, milk, and meat in arid regions.

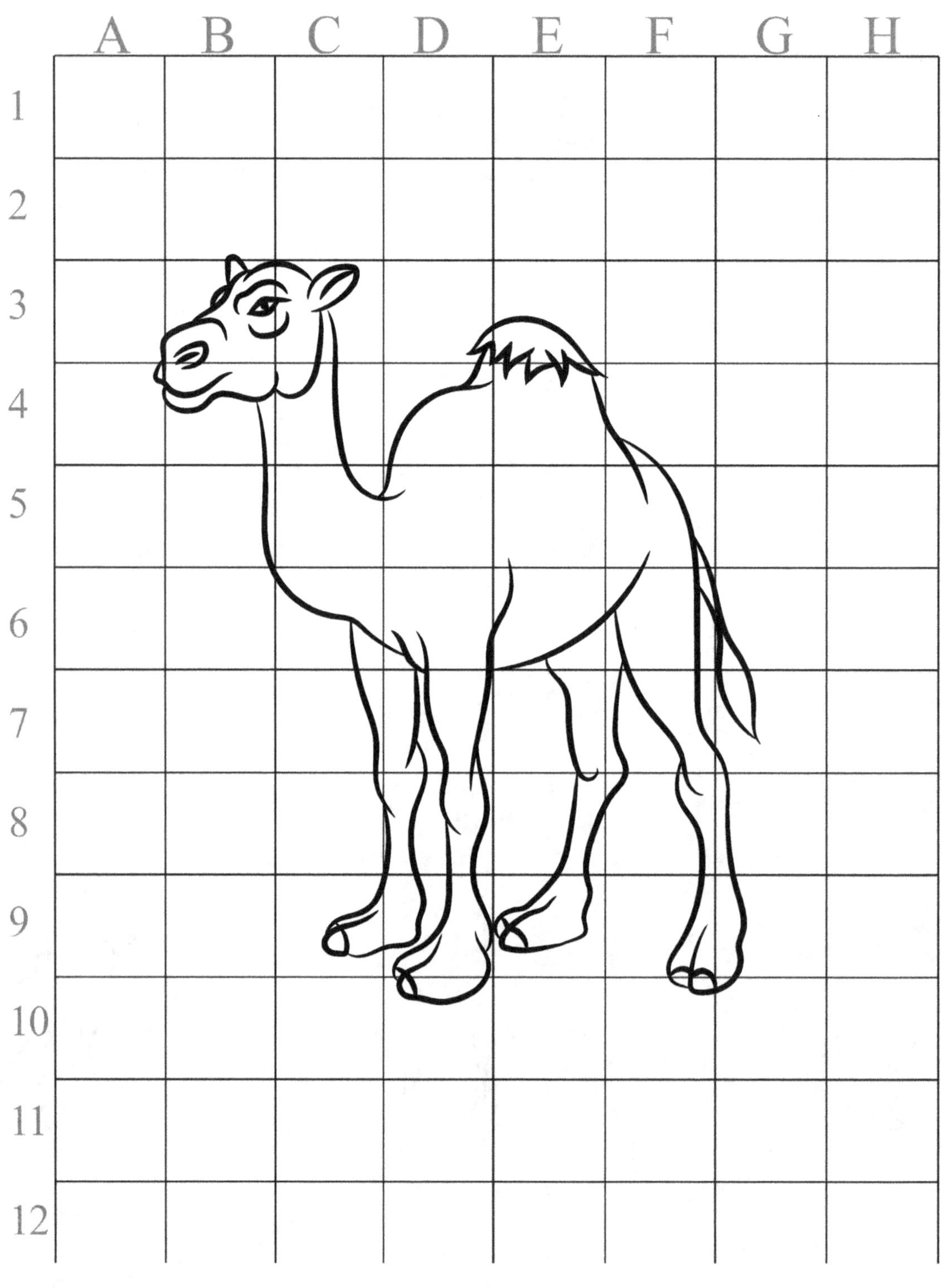

15. Enlarging the eyes
of your characters
can make them look
more childlike.

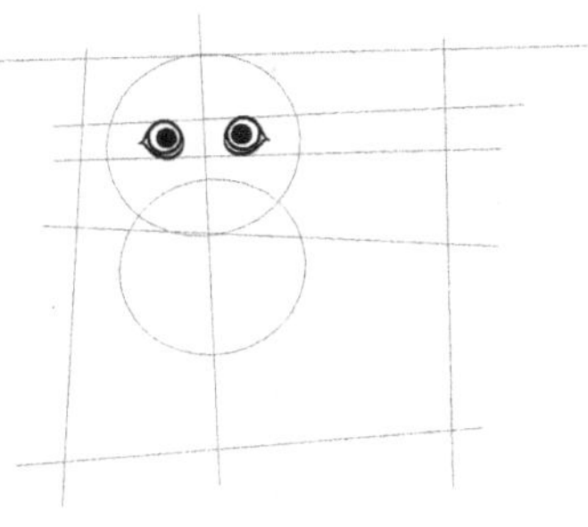

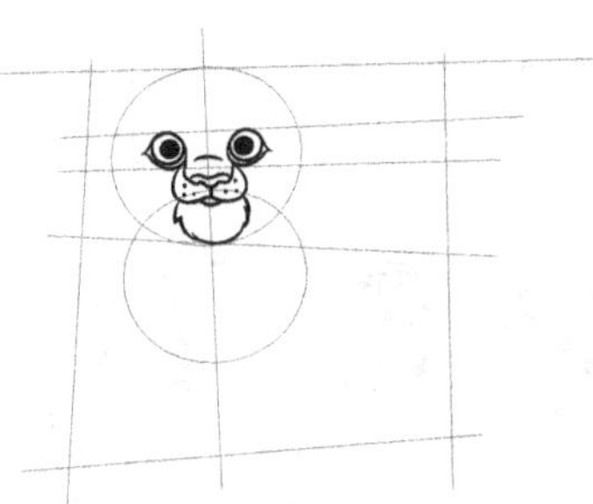

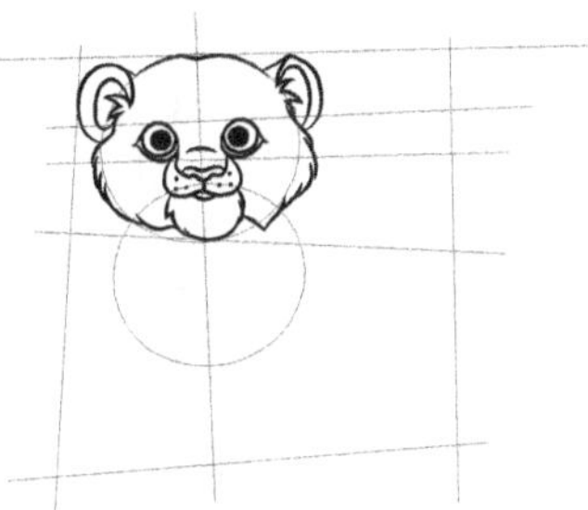

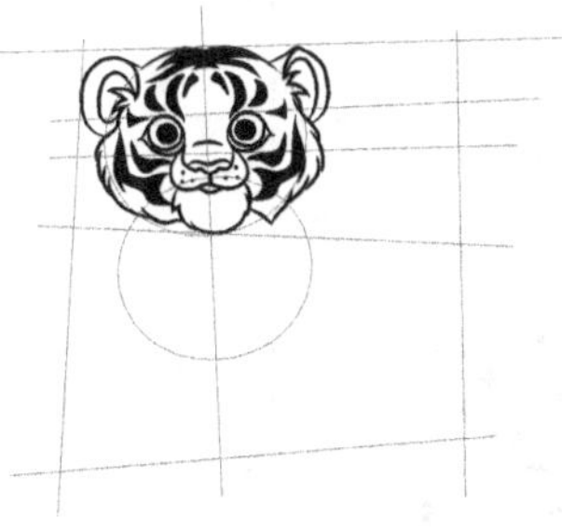

Tigers are the largest cats in the world, known for their powerful build, distinctive orange coat with black stripes, and keen hunting abilities. They are solitary hunters, capable of taking down prey much larger than themselves. Tigers are critically endangered due to habitat loss and poaching for their body parts.

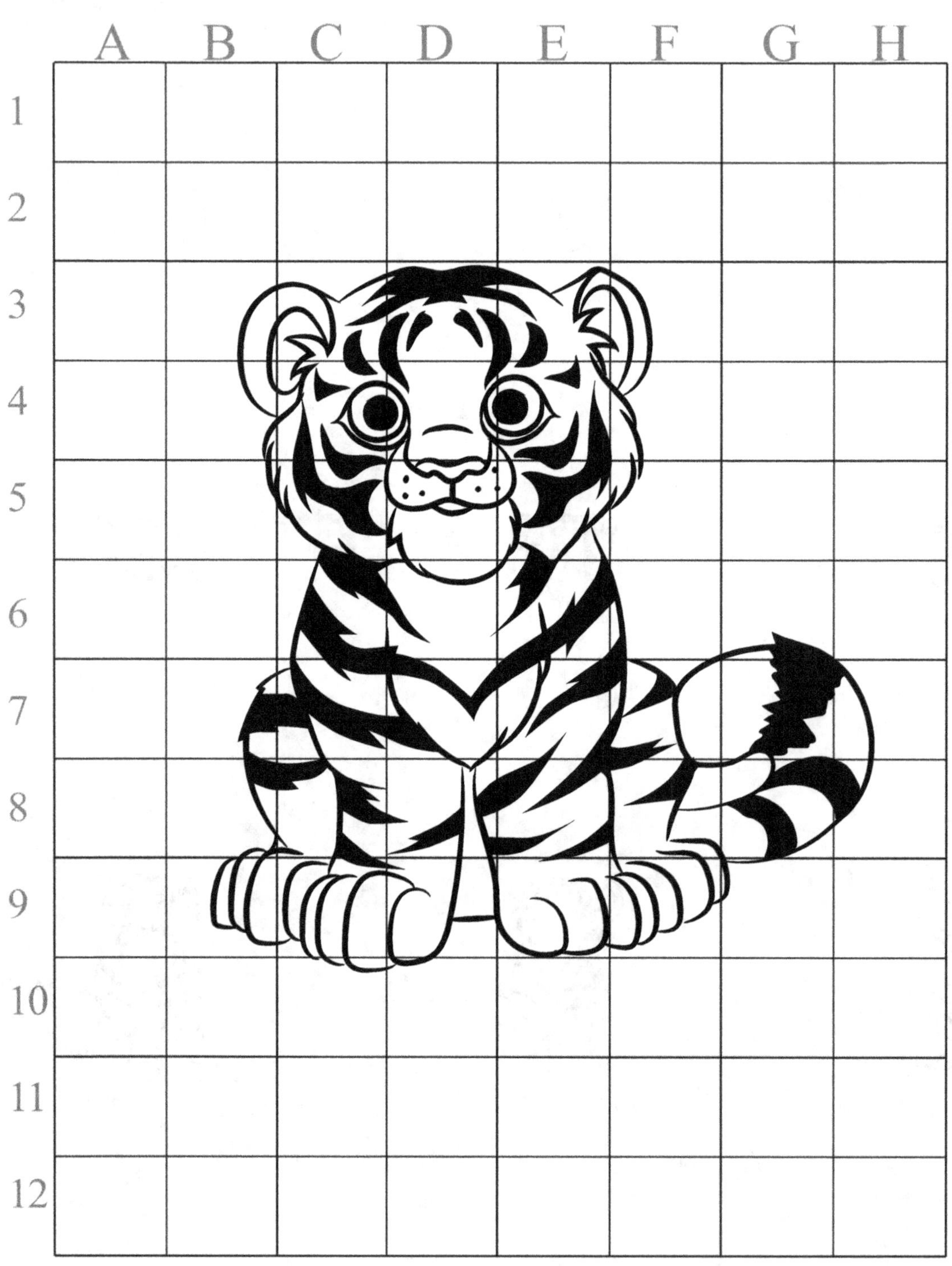

16. Anthropomorphism occurs when you give your non-human character human-like characteristics.

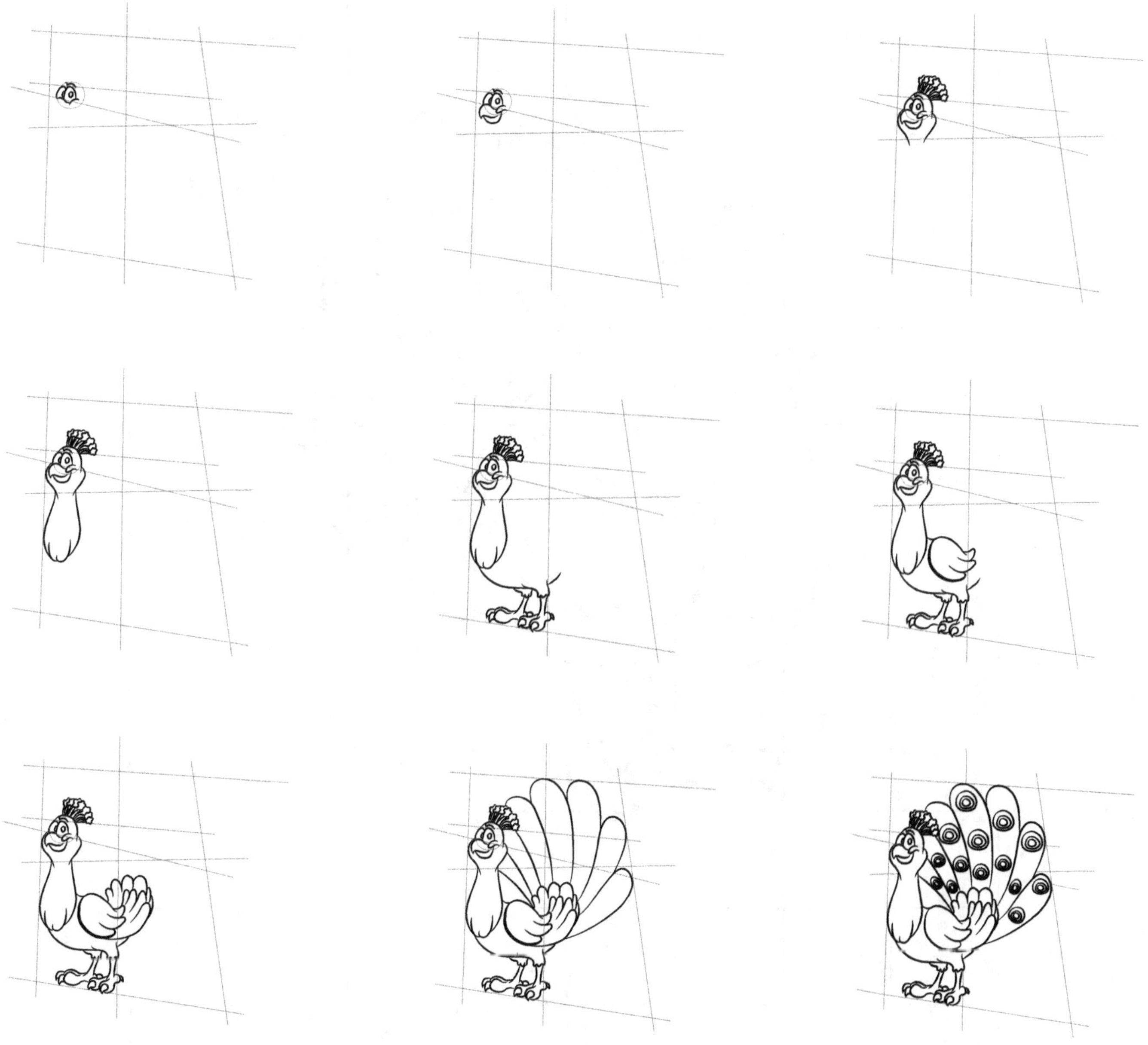

Peacocks are known for their extravagant plumage, especially the male peafowl with its colorful tail feathers, used in courtship displays to attract mates. They are native to South Asia but are also found in other parts of the world due to introductions. Peacocks are symbols of beauty and grace in many cultures.

17. There is no right way to draw a grid. It is a simple rough outline to get you started.

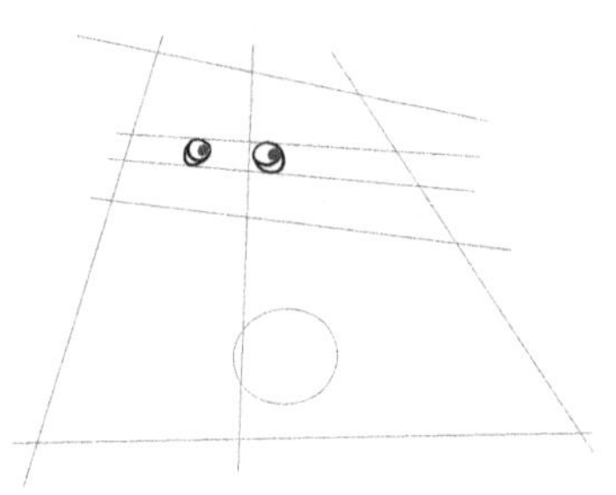 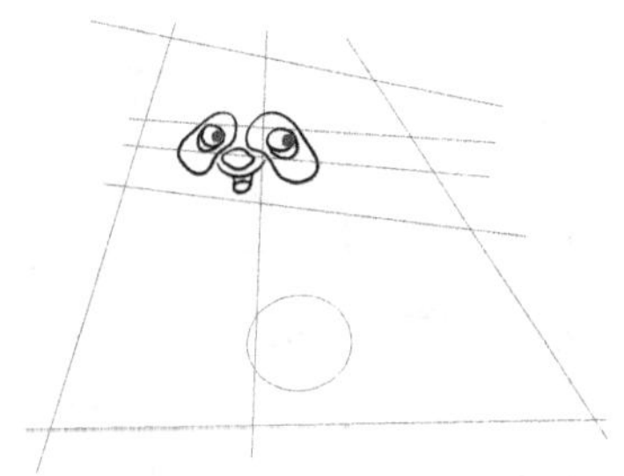 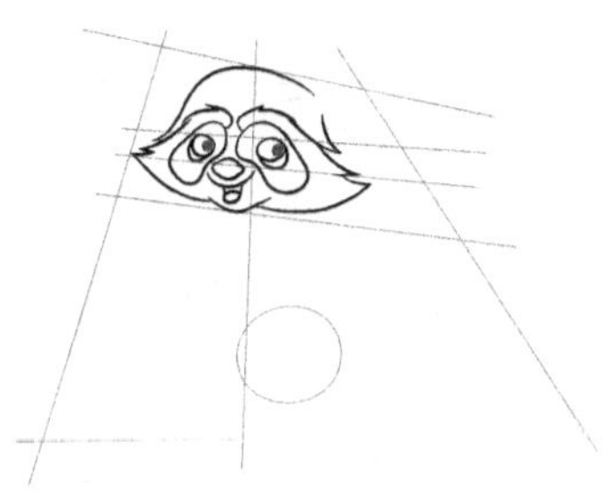

Draw you own grids or use one inch grid paper to copy this picture.

18. Building a basic
stick character can often
be a useful way to get
yourself started.

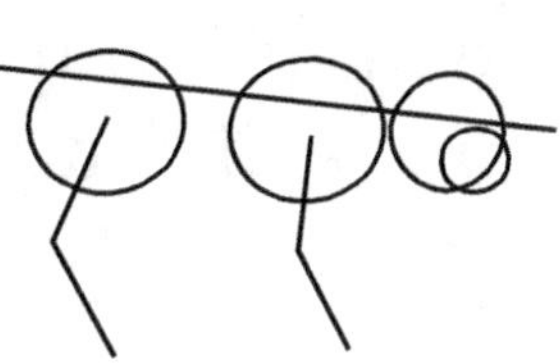

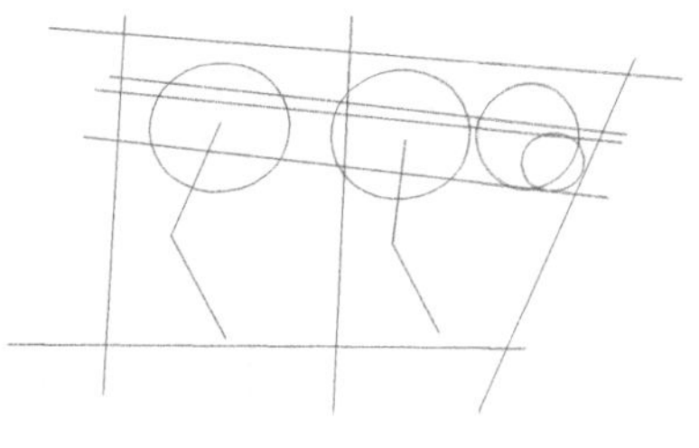

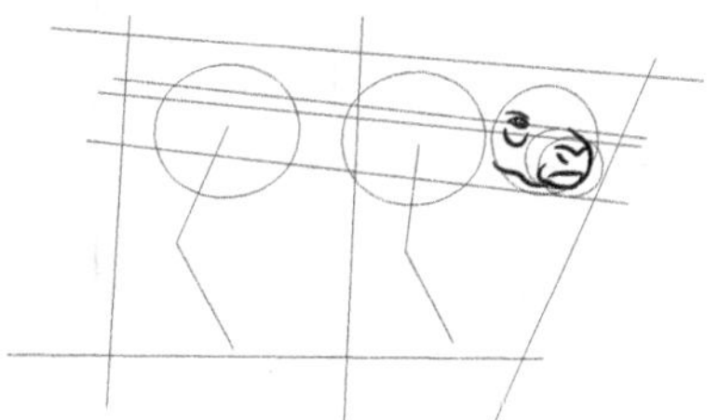

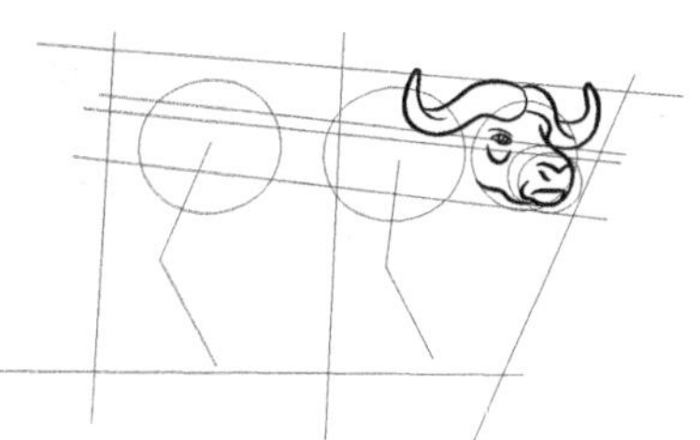

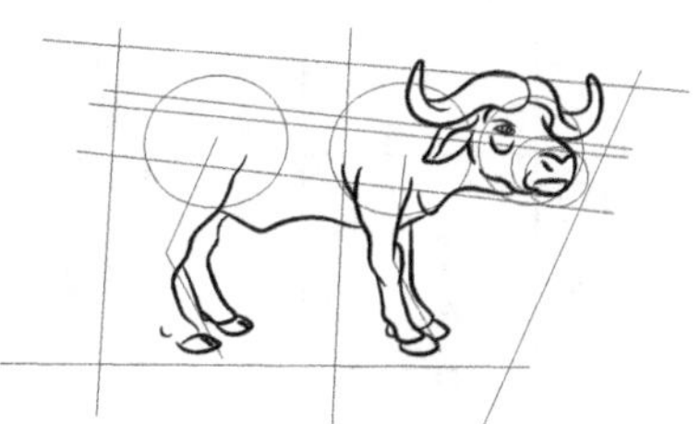

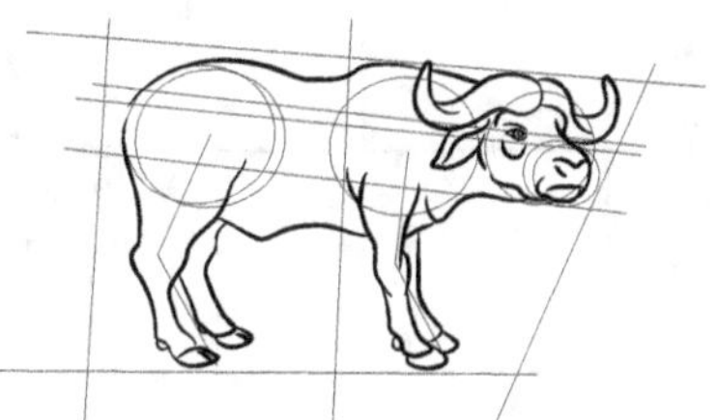

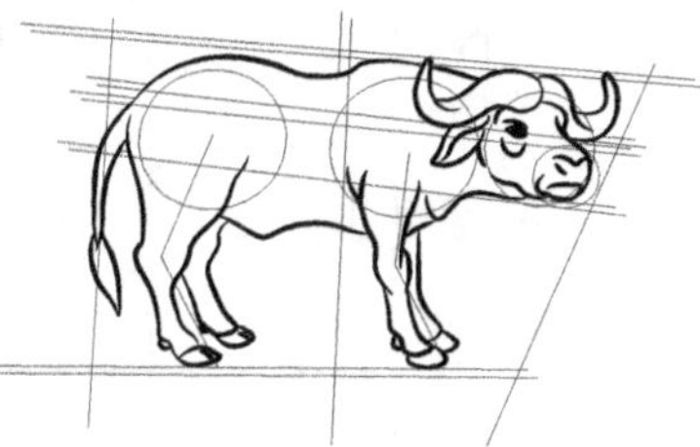

Bulls are mature male cattle known for their strength and muscular build. They are often used in agriculture for breeding purposes and in some cultures for events like bullfighting. Bulls play a significant role in livestock farming and have cultural symbolism associated with virility and power.

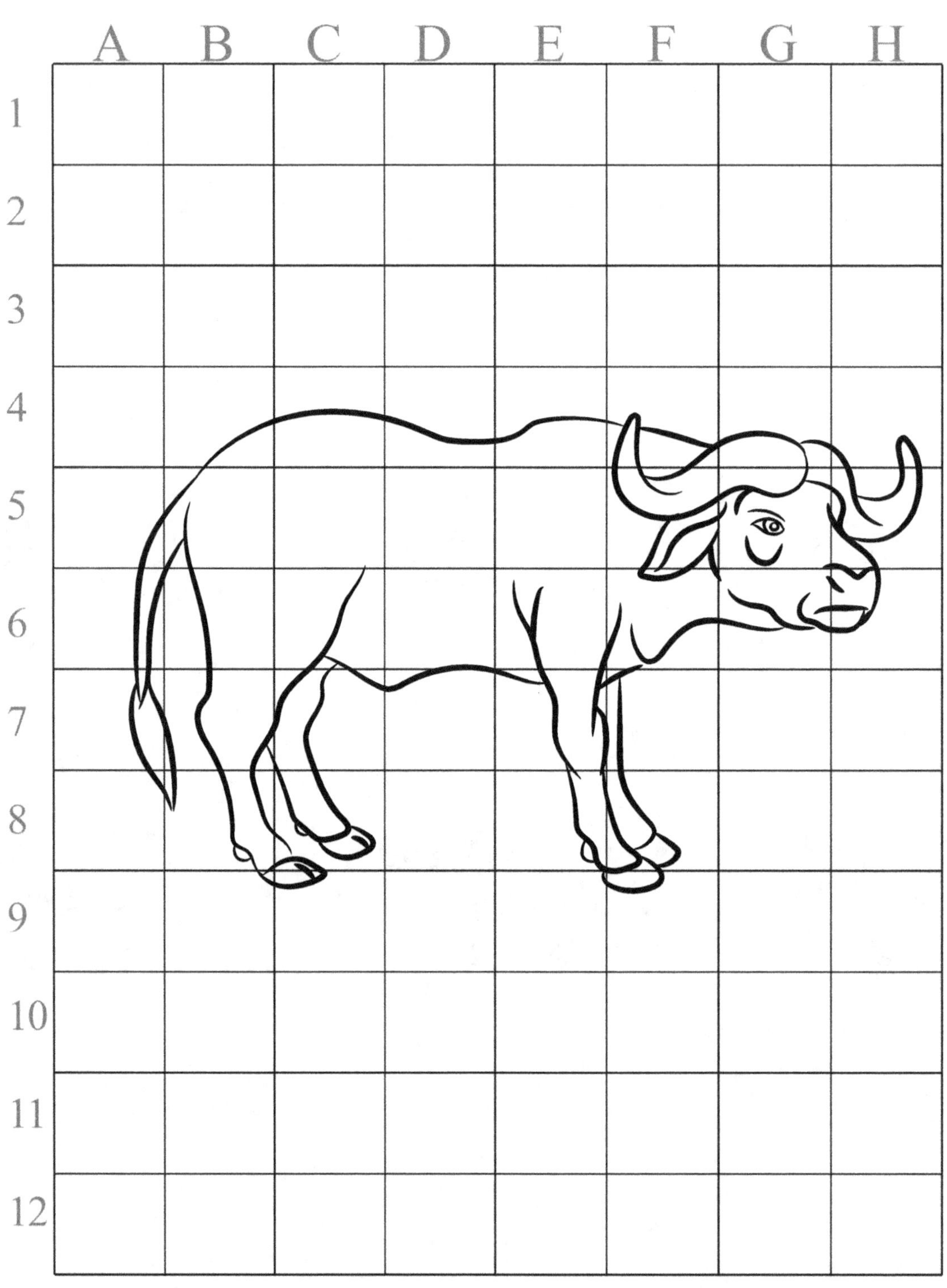

19. Enlarging the eyes of your characters can make them look more childlike and vulnerable.

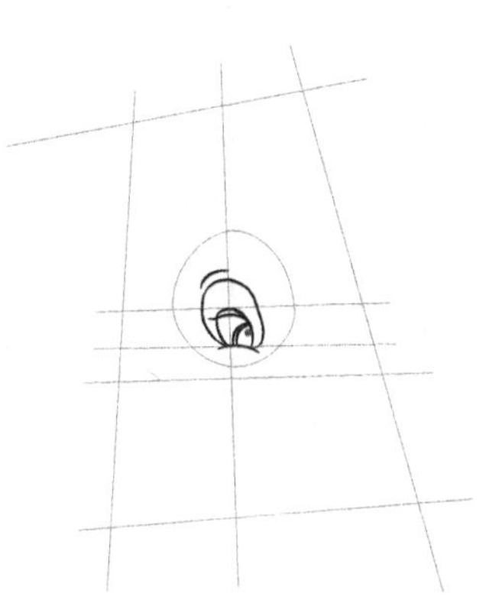

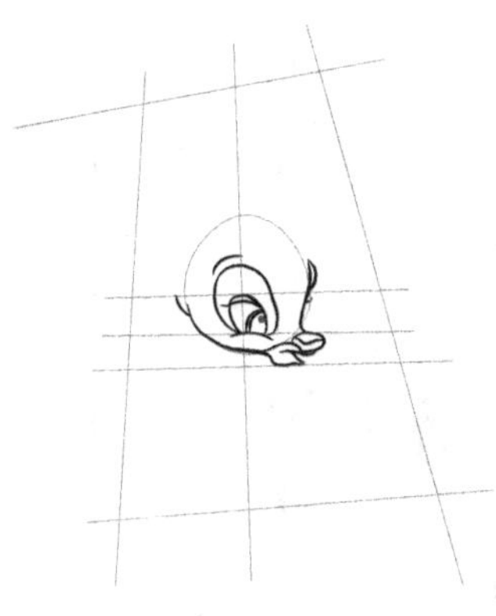

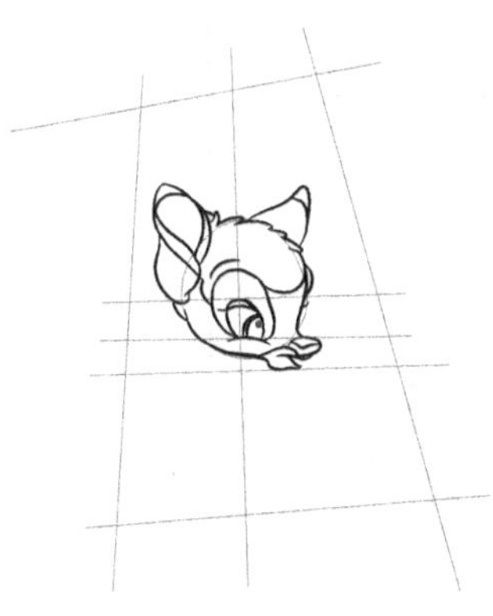

Deer are graceful herbivorous mammals found worldwide, often known for their antlers (in males of most species) used for defense, dominance, and attracting mates. They play essential roles in ecosystems as herbivores and are admired for their agility and beauty.

20. Try lengthening
different parts of
your character's body
to create a range of
different effects.

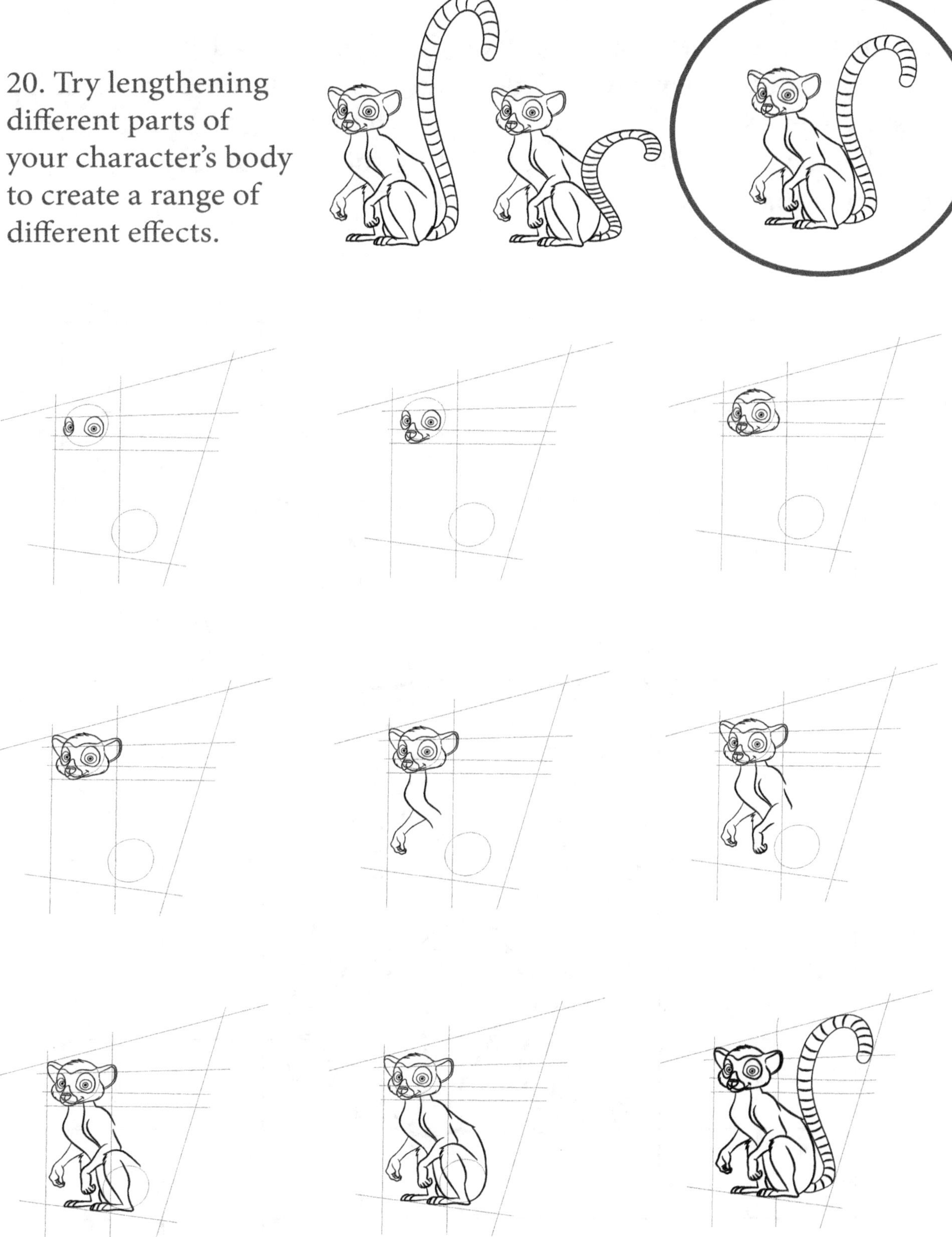

Lemurs are primates found only on the island of Madagascar and nearby islands. They have a wide range of species, some of which have distinctive striped tails. Lemurs are known for their unique adaptations and behaviors, making them fascinating subjects of study and conservation efforts.

21. Placing ellipses where you character has joints can often help when developing a plan for your character.

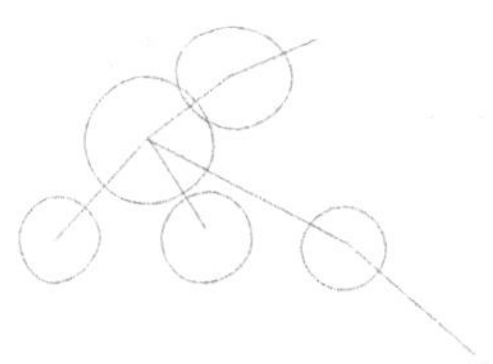

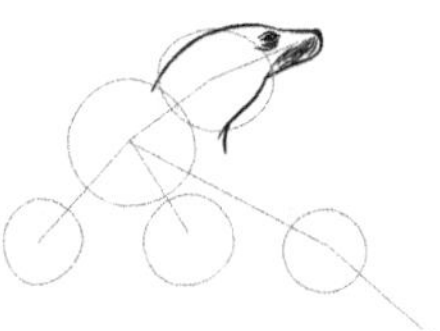

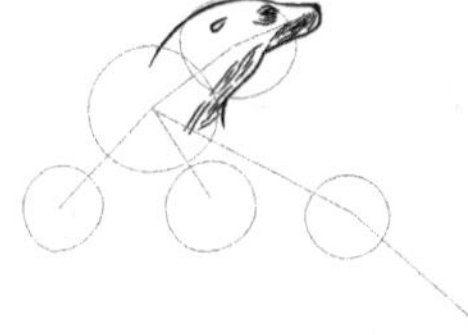

Seals are marine mammals with streamlined bodies and flippers for swimming. They inhabit oceans worldwide, coming ashore to breed and molt. Seals feed on fish and squid and are known for their playful behavior and ability to bask on beaches or ice floes.

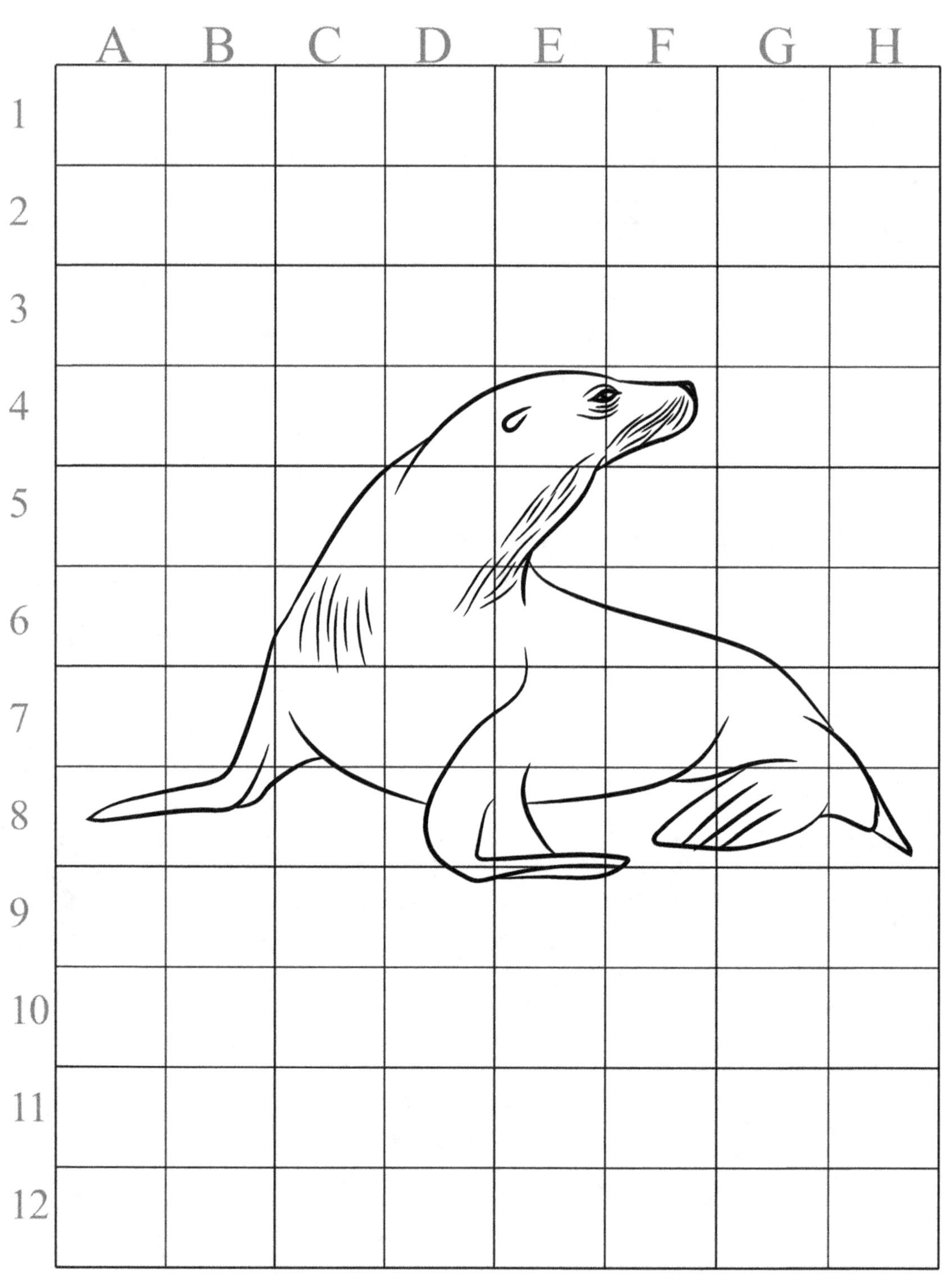

22. Small changes to your character's mouth can make a big difference to their emotional expression.

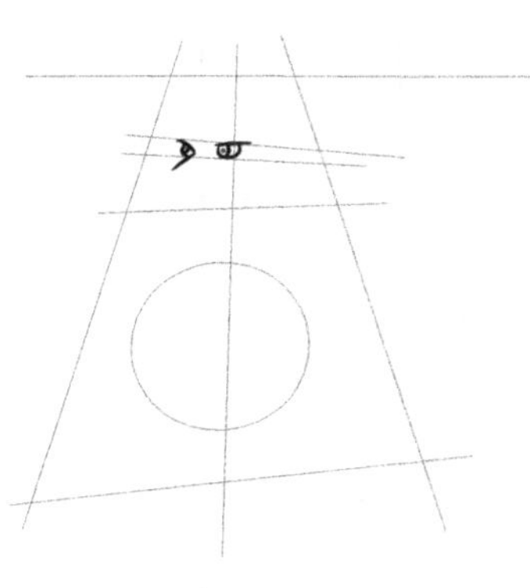 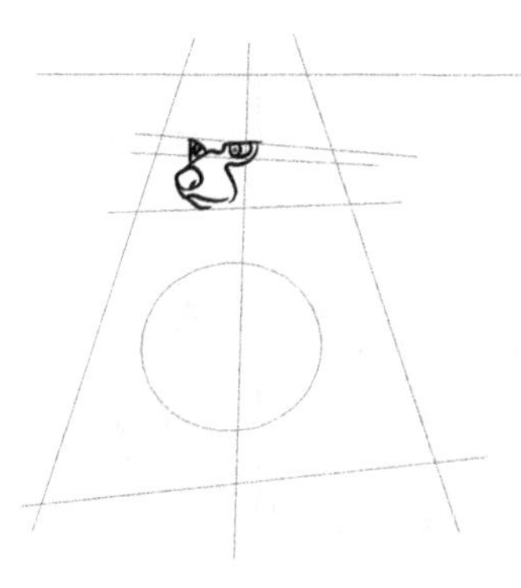 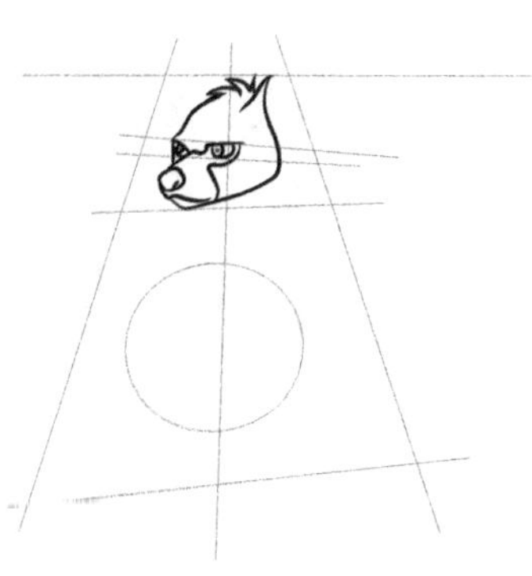

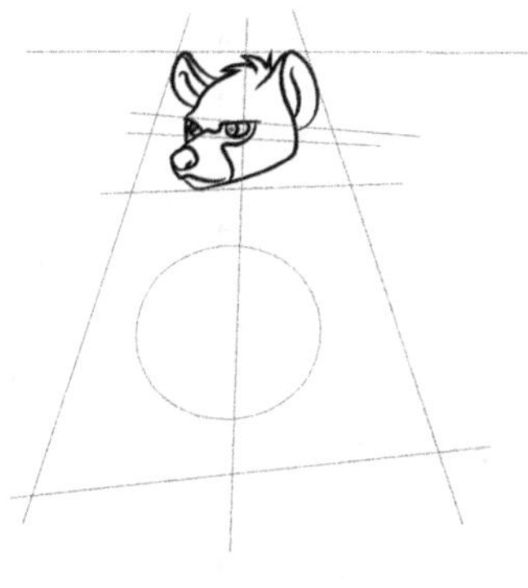 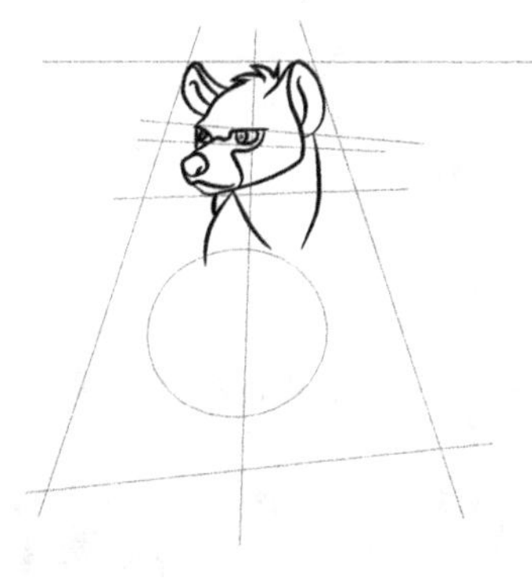 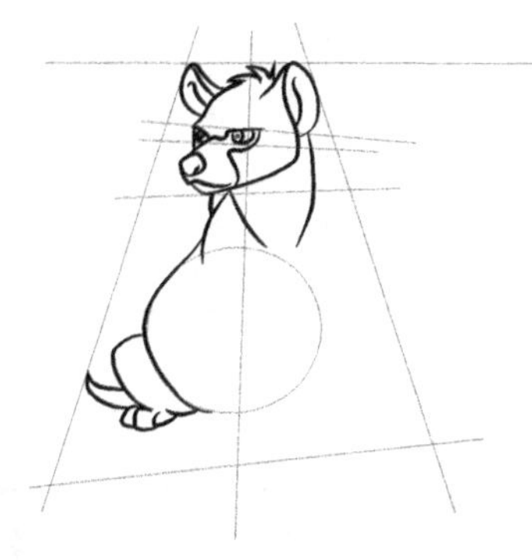

Hyenas are carnivorous mammals known for their distinct laughs, powerful jaws, and scavenging abilities. They live in clans led by females and inhabit savannas and grasslands in Africa and parts of Asia. Hyenas are skilled hunters and opportunistic feeders, playing crucial roles in their ecosystems as both predators and scavengers.

23. Give your character a curved look with the use of an ellipse.

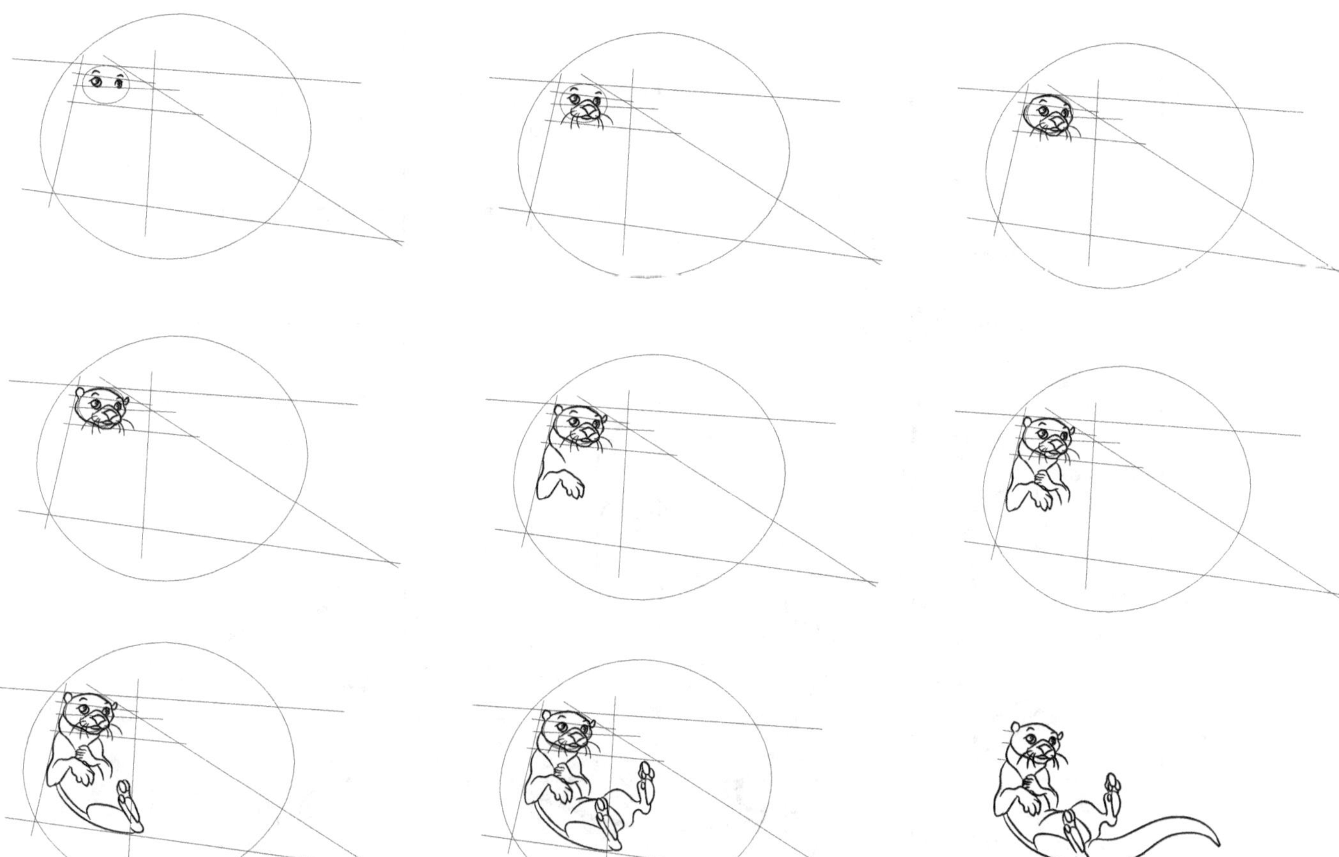

Otters are aquatic mammals known for their playful behavior and streamlined bodies adapted for swimming. They are found in rivers, lakes, and coastal waters worldwide. Otters are skilled hunters, feeding on fish, crustaceans, and other aquatic creatures. They use their dexterous paws to manipulate food and are social animals, often seen in family groups.

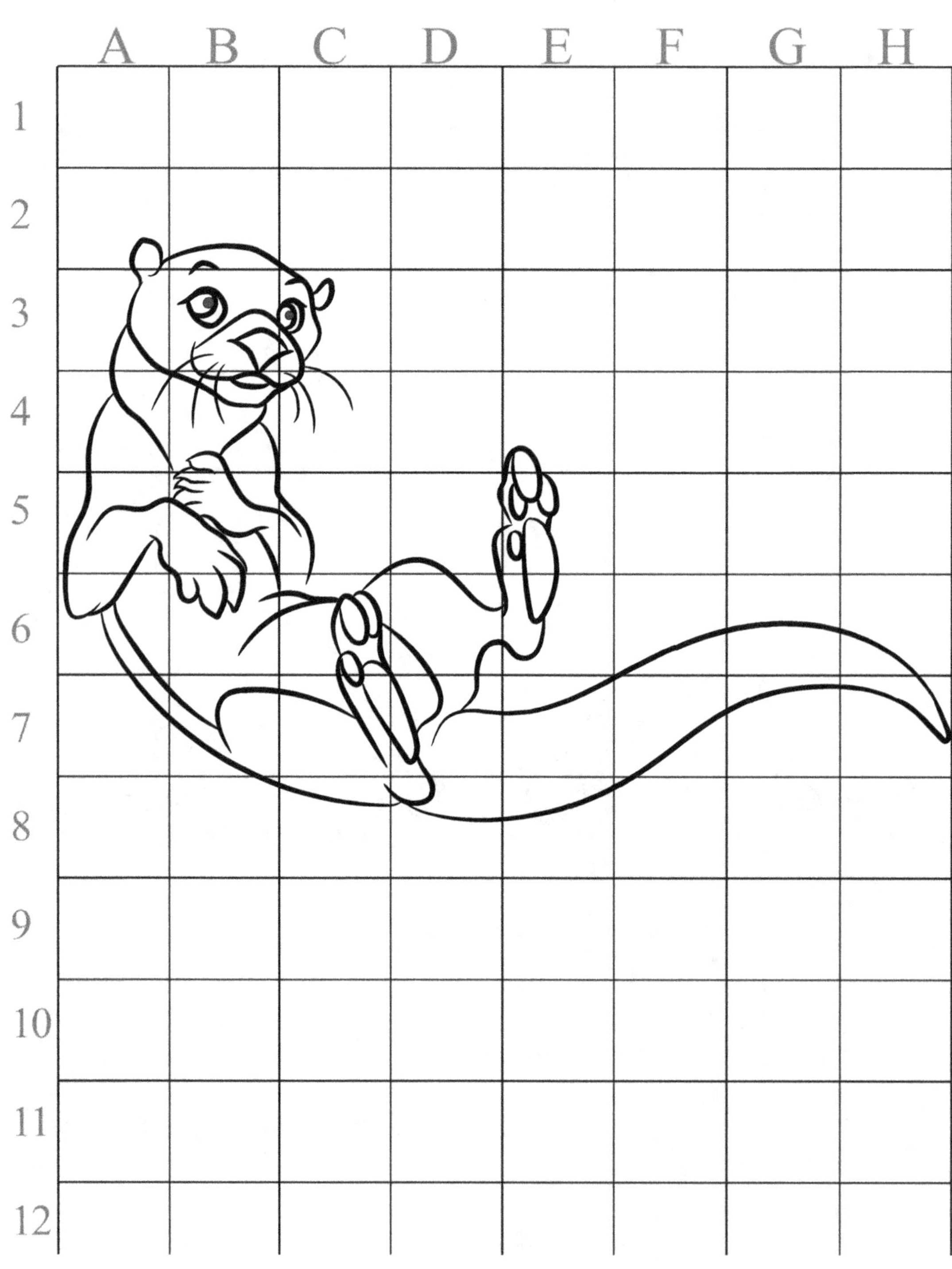

24. A grid will help you decide where the important parts of your character need to be.

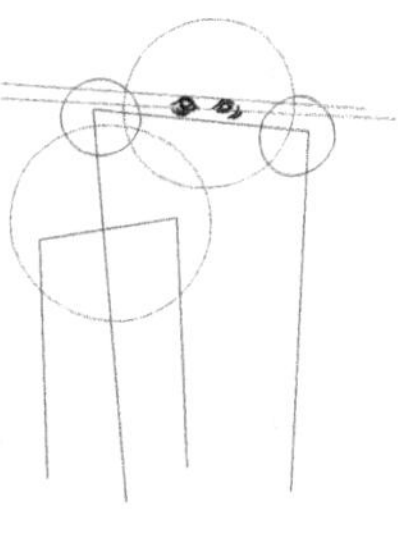
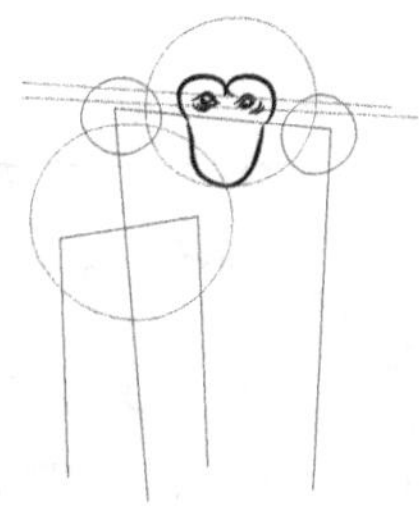
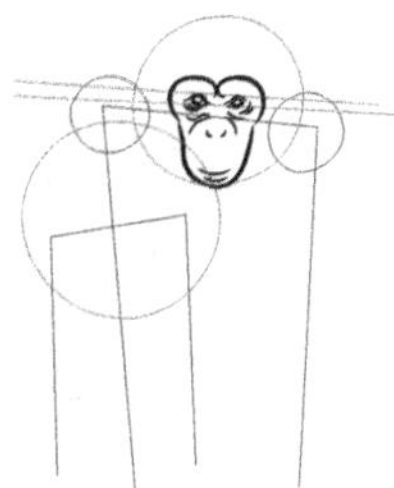

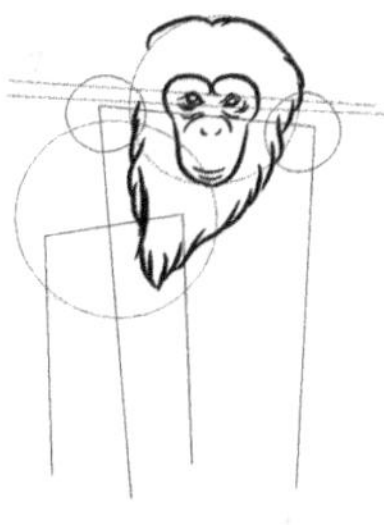

Chimpanzees, or chimps, are highly intelligent primates native to Africa. They live in social groups led by alpha males and exhibit tool use, communication through gestures and vocalizations, and complex social behaviors. Chimpanzees are omnivorous, eating fruits, leaves, insects, and occasionally hunting small animals.

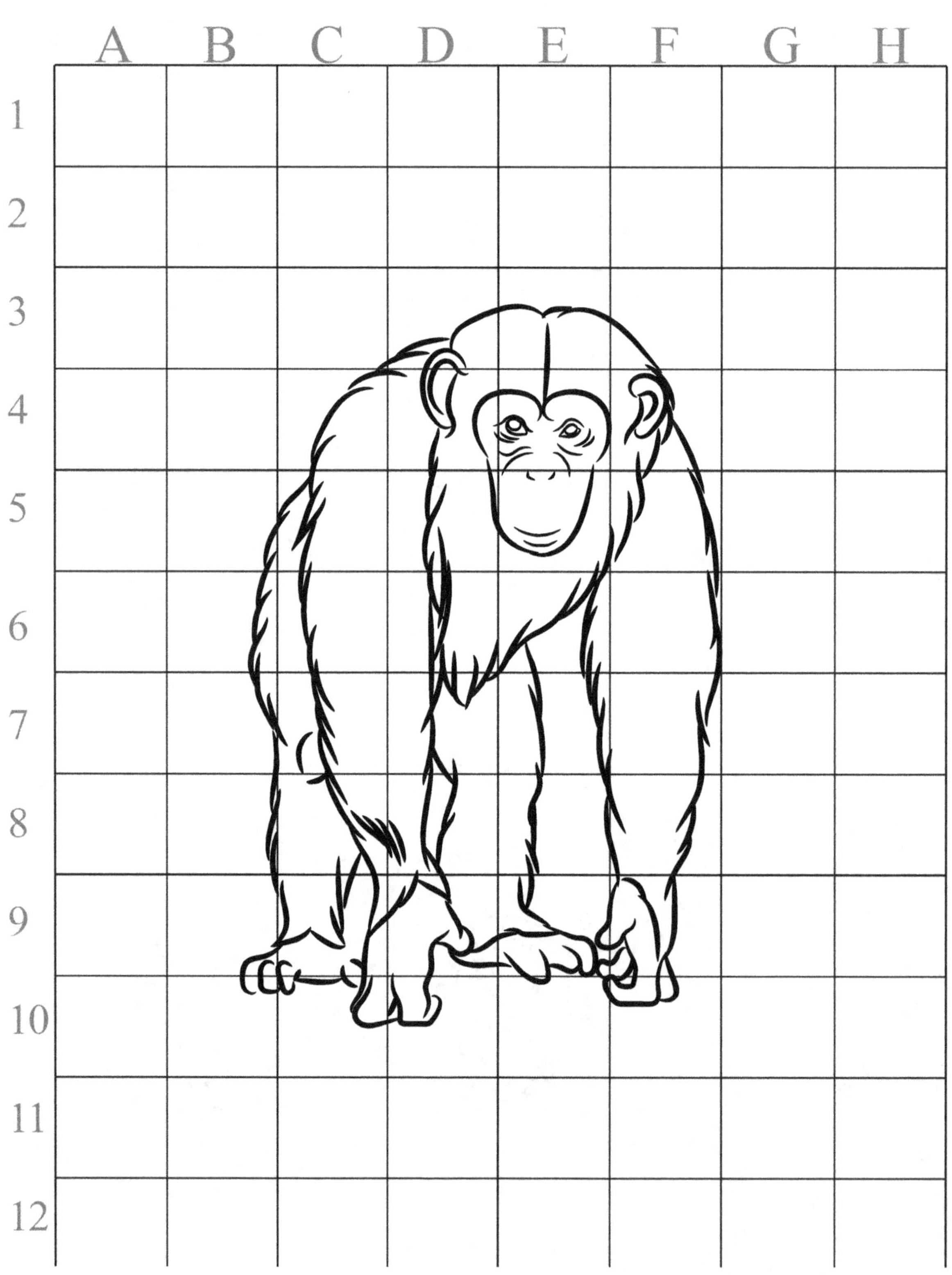

25. You can build your character around
rough outlines created in your grid.

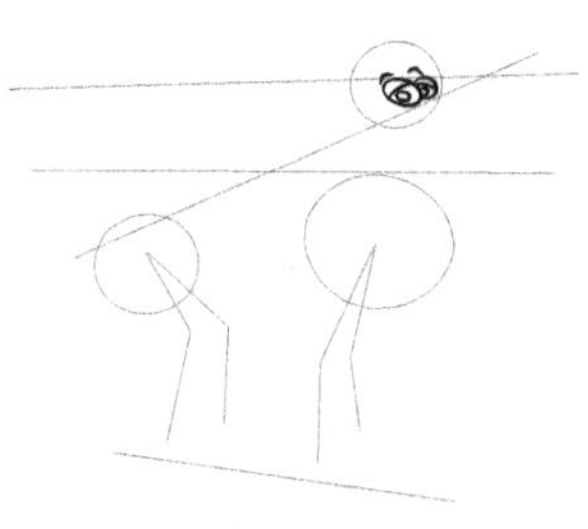 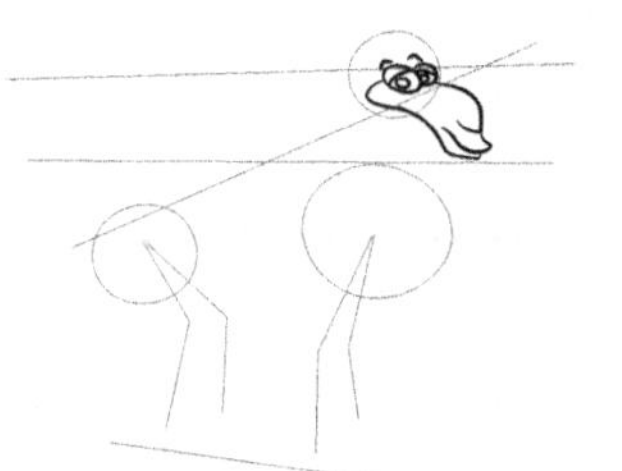 

Llamas are domesticated South American camelids known for their woolly coats and long necks. They are used as pack animals in the Andes Mountains and are prized for their fiber, meat, and even as therapy animals. Llamas are social, intelligent creatures with gentle dispositions.

26. There is no right way to draw a grid. It is a
simple rough outline to get you started.

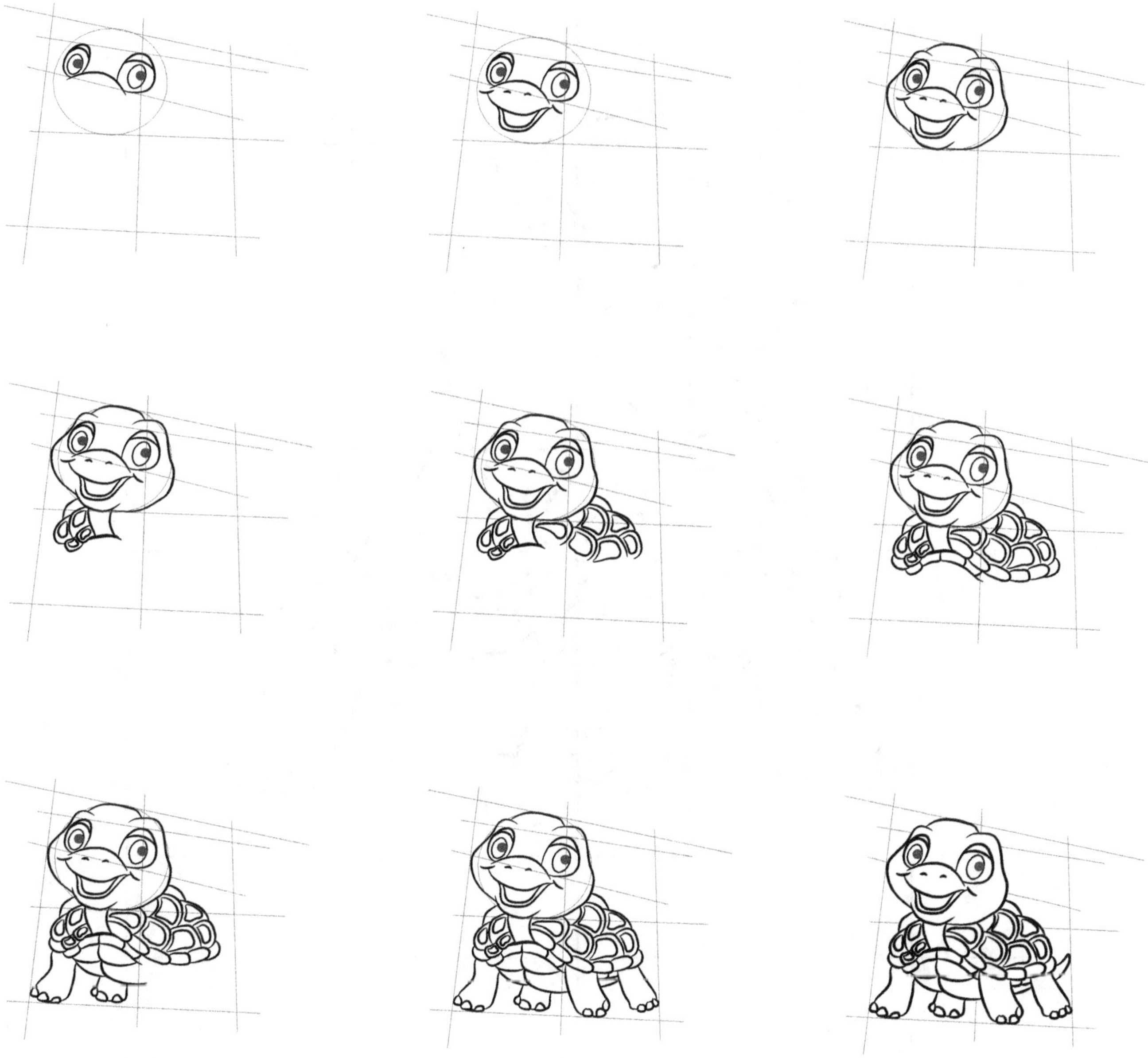

Tortoises are land-dwelling reptiles known for their long lifespans and hard, domed shells. They are herbivores, primarily eating grasses and leafy plants. Tortoises are found in diverse habitats, from deserts to tropical forests. They are slow-moving but have remarkable resilience and can live for over a century.

27. Separate your grid into sections to help you decide how you want to proportion your drawing. This can help you to alter the height of your character.

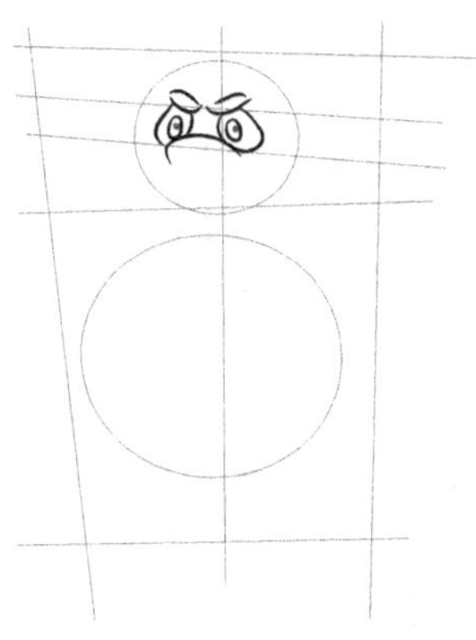

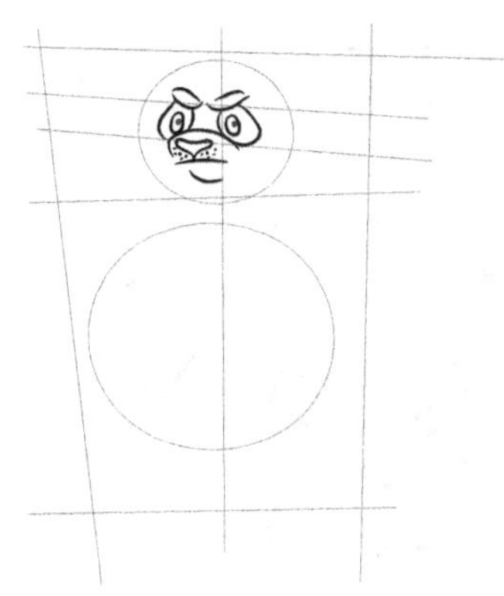

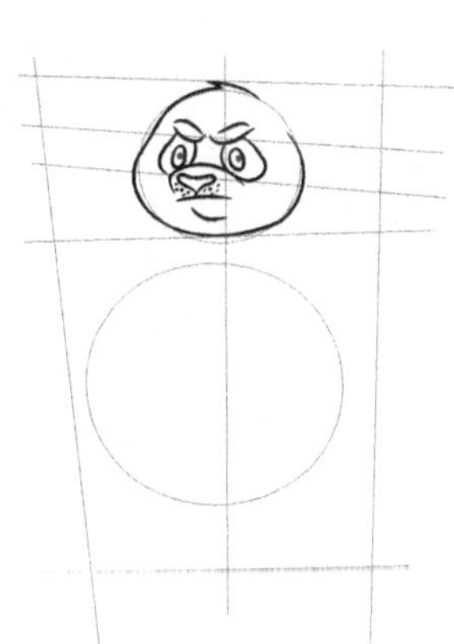

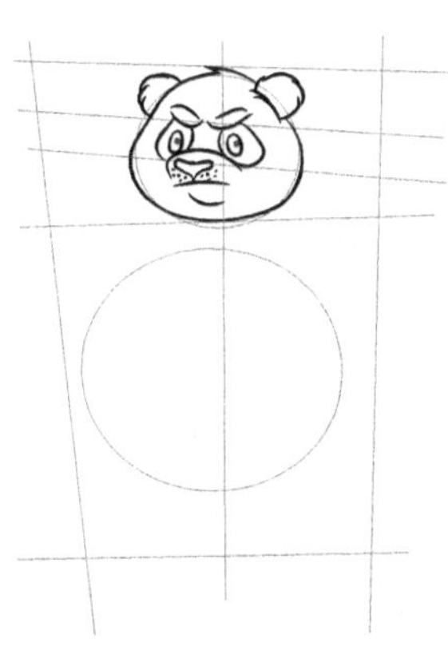

Black bears are medium-sized bears native to North America. They have a versatile diet, consuming fruits, nuts, insects, small mammals, and carrion. Known for their climbing abilities, black bears inhabit forests, swamps, and mountainous regions. They are generally solitary and hibernate during winter, with mothers giving birth to cubs in their dens.

28. The more information you can fit on your initial grid, the easier it will be to structure your drawing.

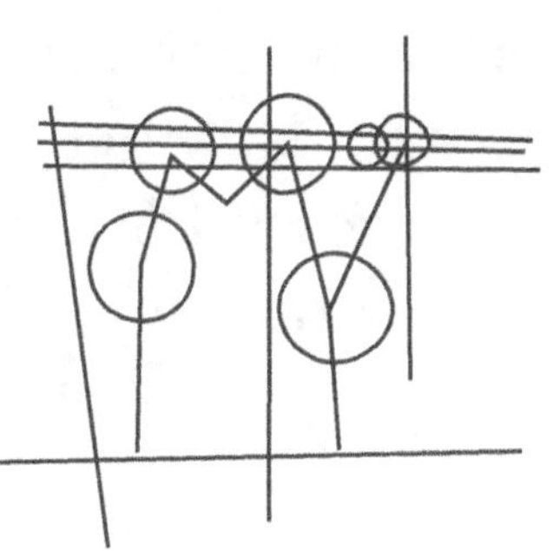

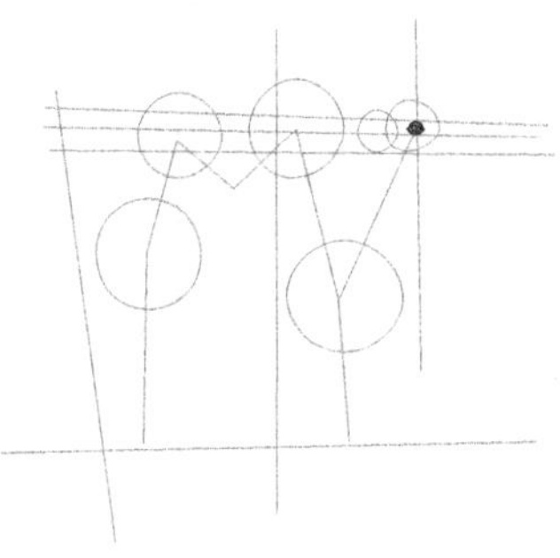

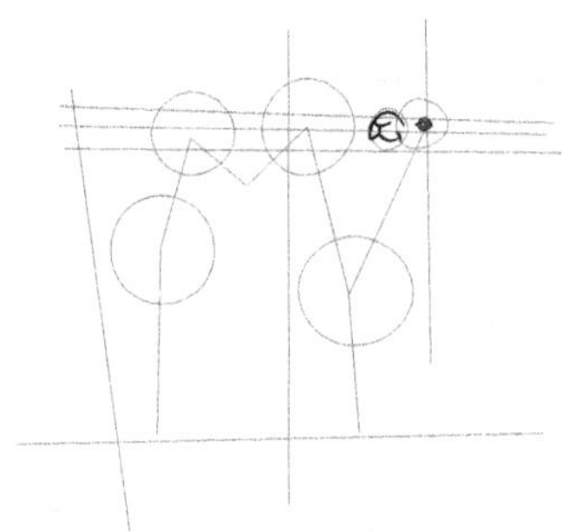

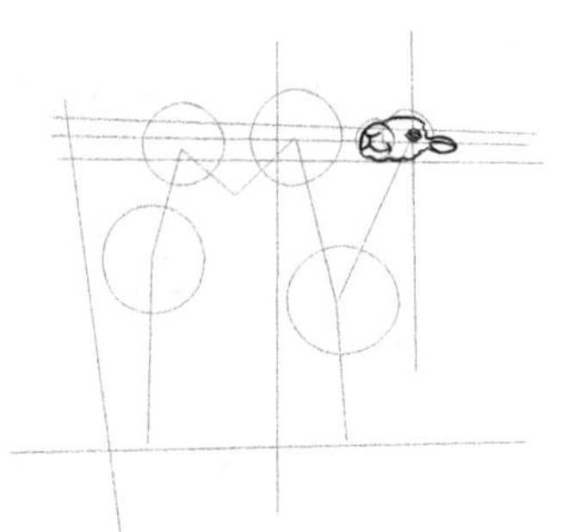

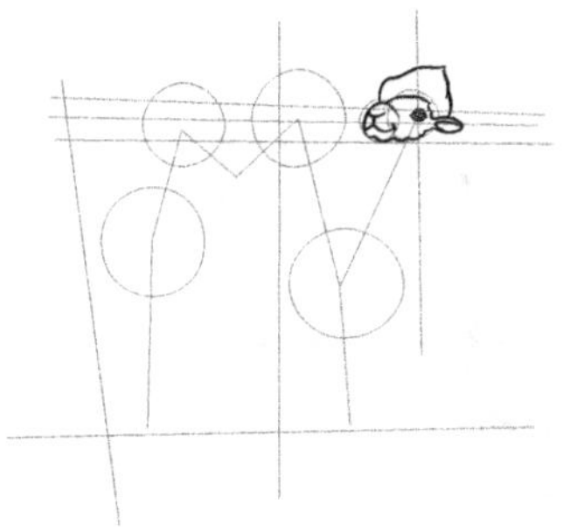

The Bactrian camel, is native to Central Asia. Adapted to harsh climates, it can survive extreme temperatures and long periods without water. Bactrian camels are known for their two humps, which store fat for energy. They are used for transportation, wool, and milk by nomadic cultures.

29. The use of overlapping ellipses can be very useful when you are drawing characters that are looking out of your page.

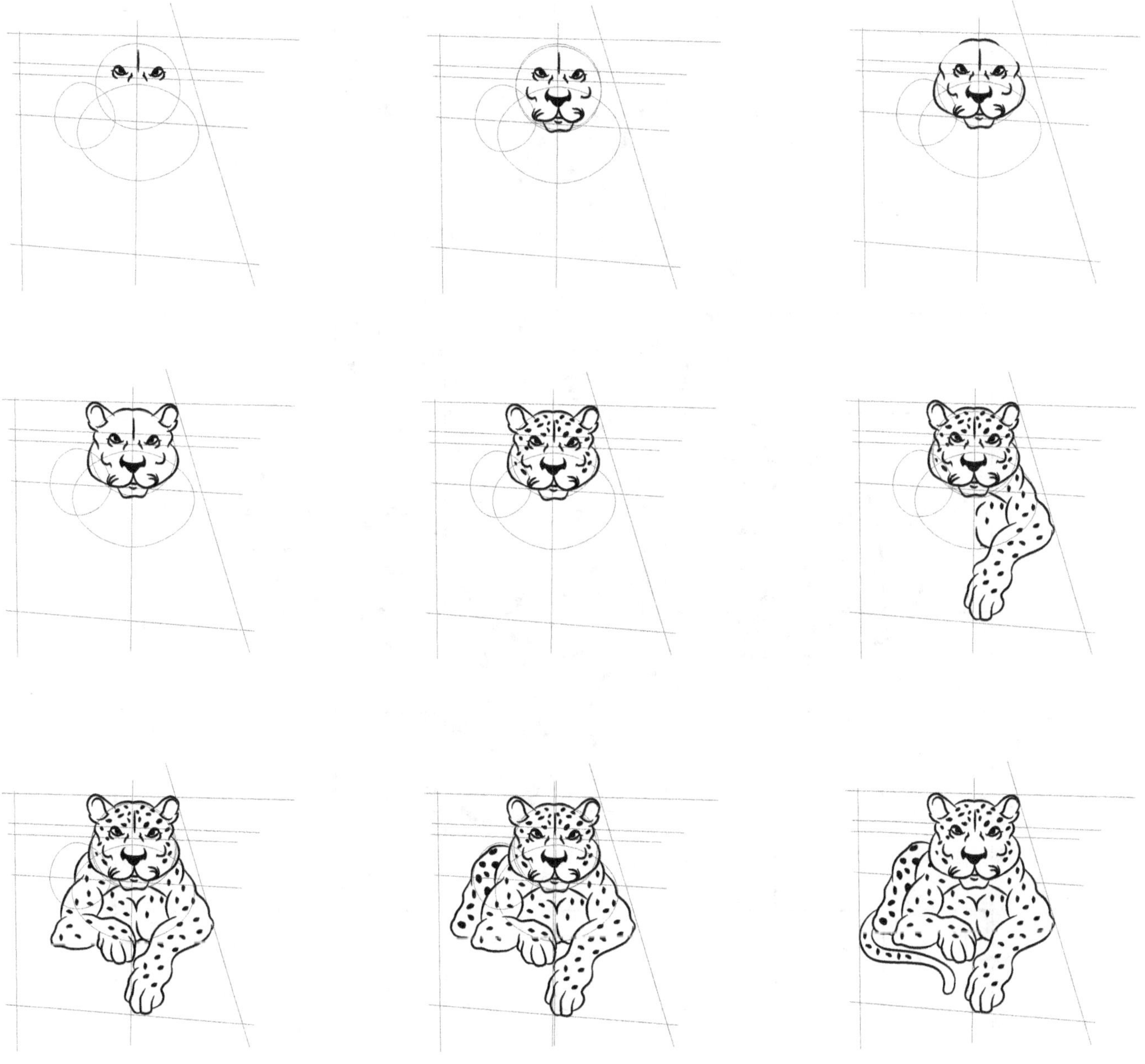

Leopards are versatile big cats found in Africa and parts of Asia.
Known for their distinctive spotted coats, they are excellent climbers
and can drag prey into trees. Leopards are solitary and adaptable
hunters, preying on a wide range of animals. They are elusive, making
them difficult to observe in the wild.

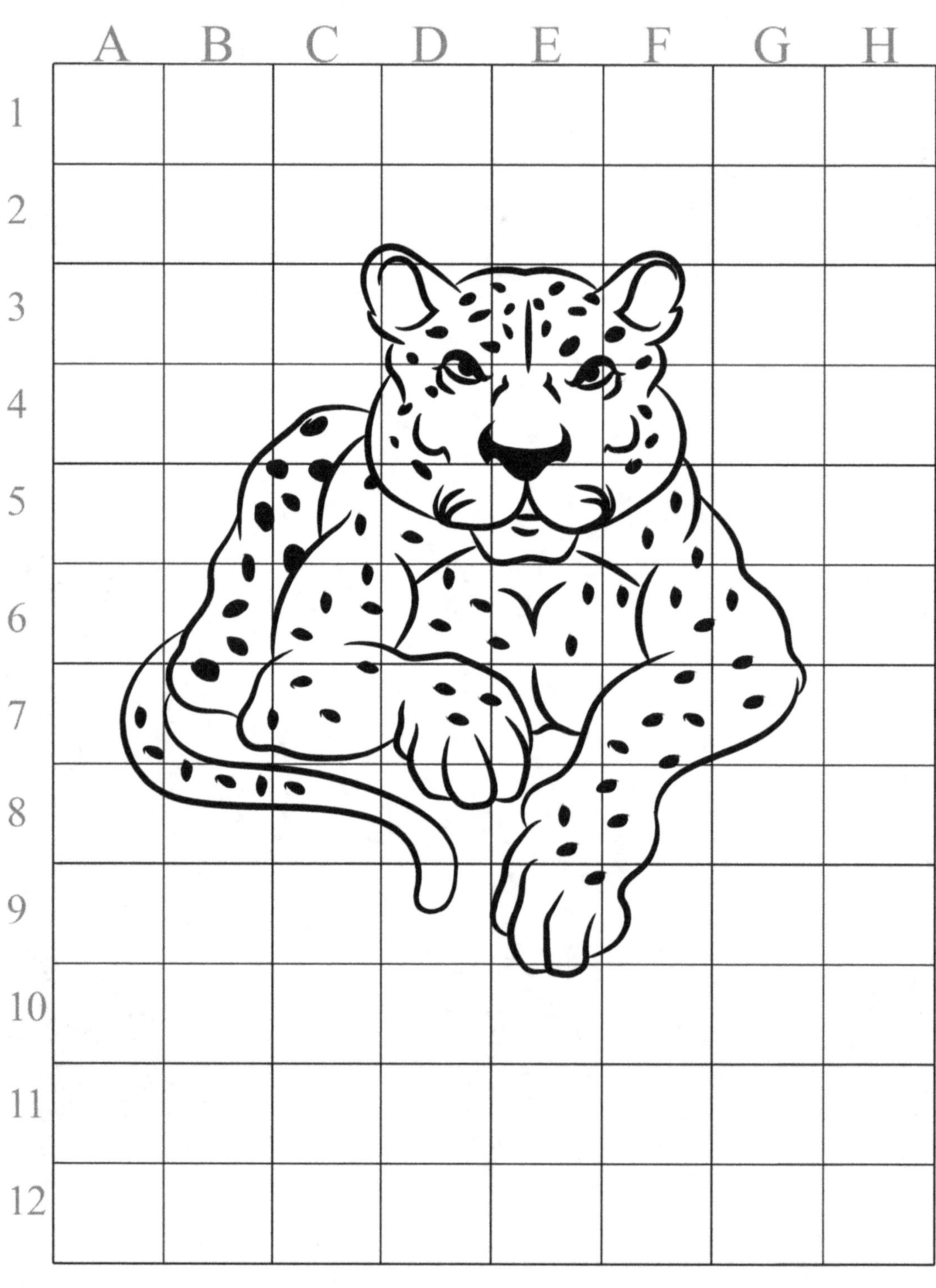

30. If you want your character to look more realistic remove human-like (anthropomorphic) features.

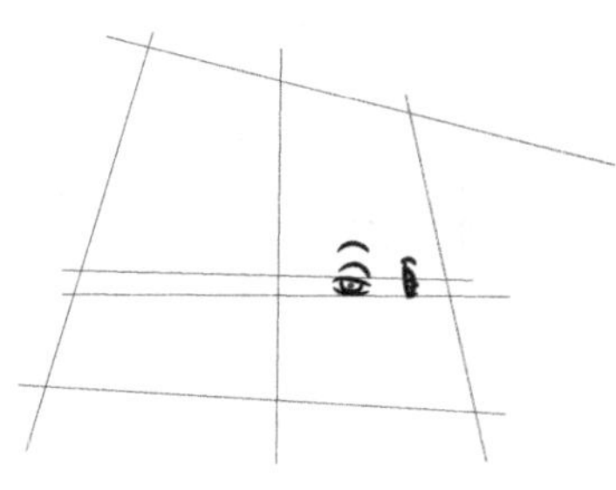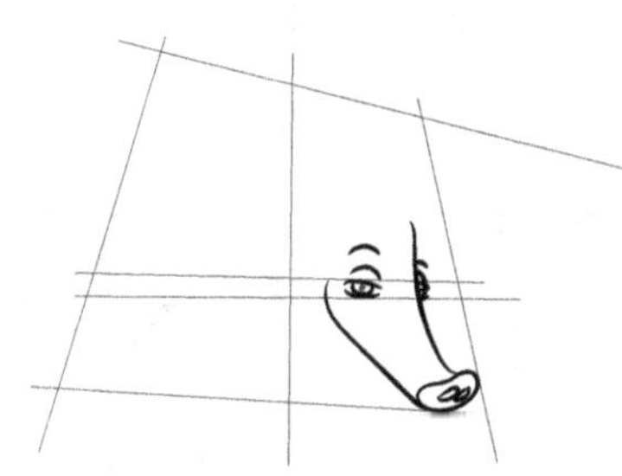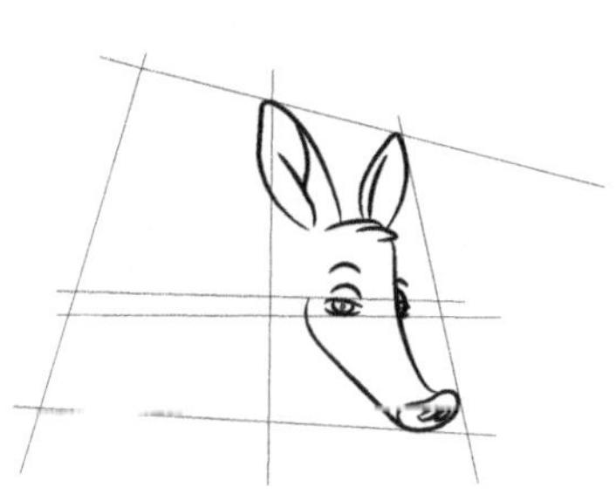

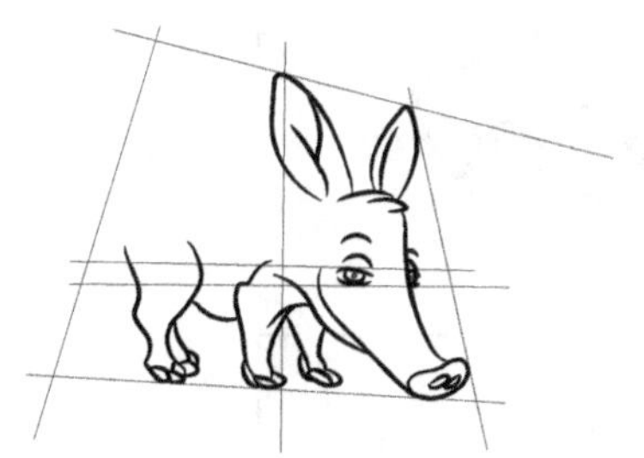

Anteaters are unique mammals known for their elongated snouts and specialized tongues, which they use to feed on ants and termites. Found in Central and South America, they have strong claws for tearing into insect nests. Anteaters are solitary animals with poor vision but an excellent sense of smell.

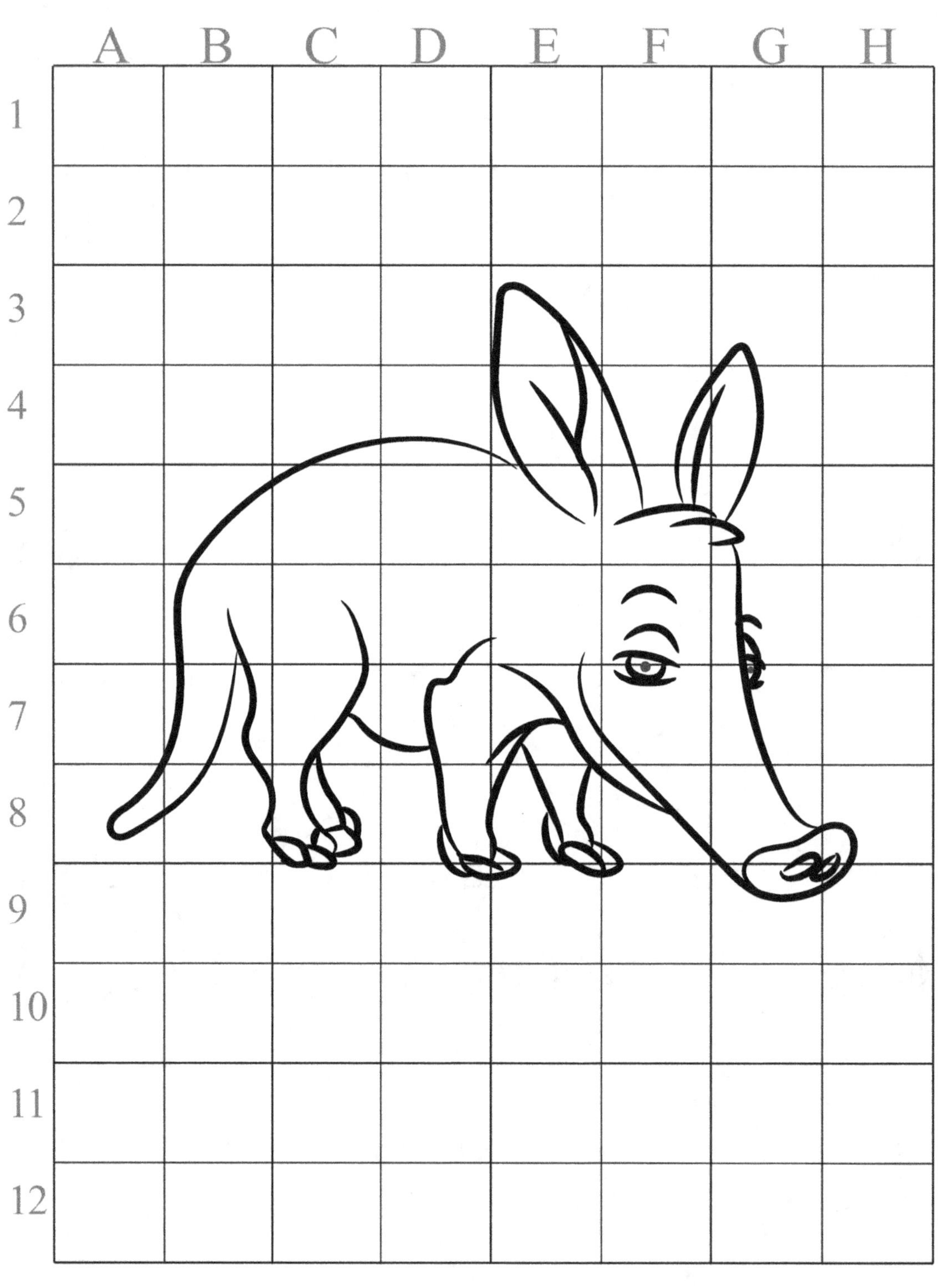

31. Add extra features to your character to make it look more original.

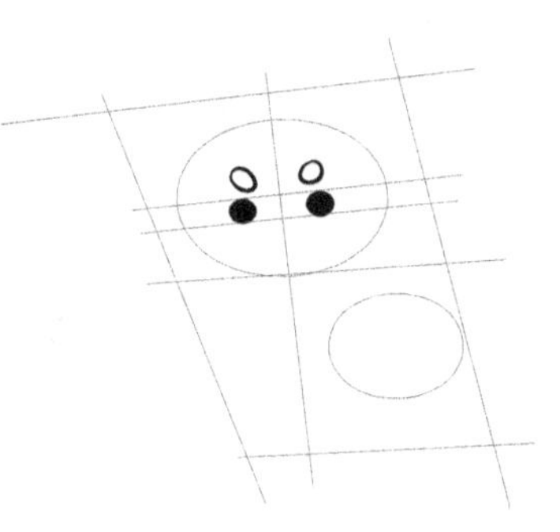
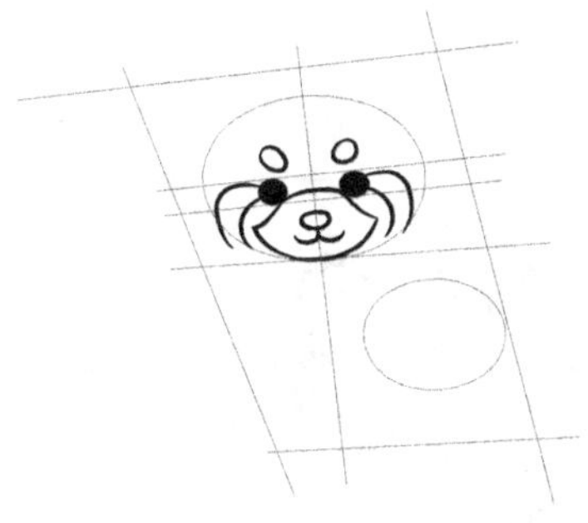

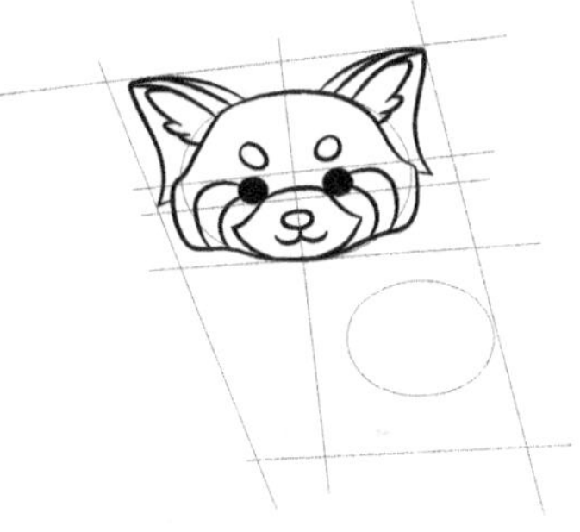

The Bearded Terrier, commonly known as the Bearded Collie, is a
herding dog breed known for its shaggy double coat and lively
personality. Originating in Scotland, these dogs are energetic,
intelligent, and affectionate, making them excellent family pets and
working dogs. They are recognized for their distinctive "beard" of long
hair under the chin.

32. The use of an ellipse in your grid can bring curvature into your drawing.

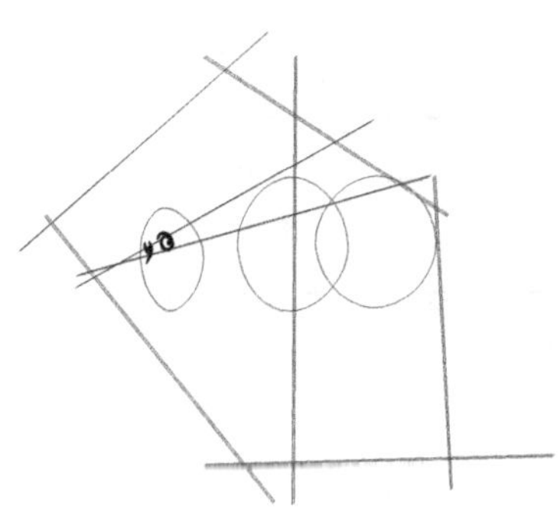
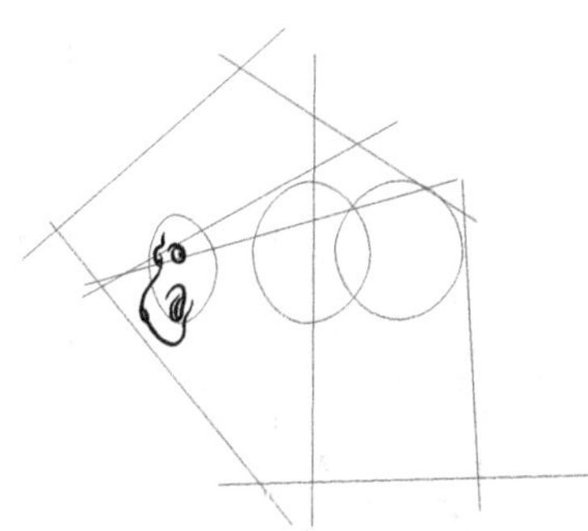
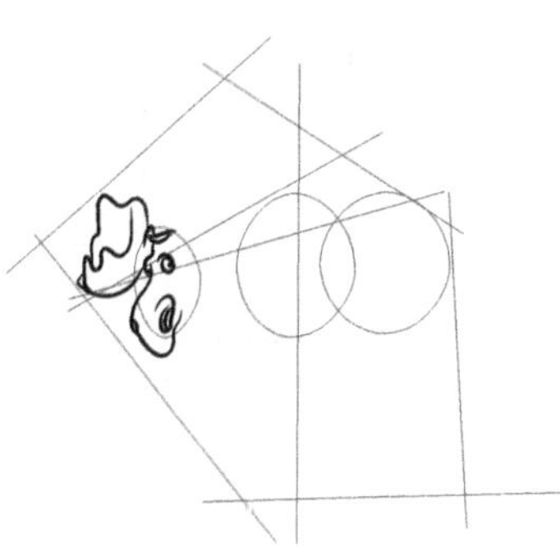

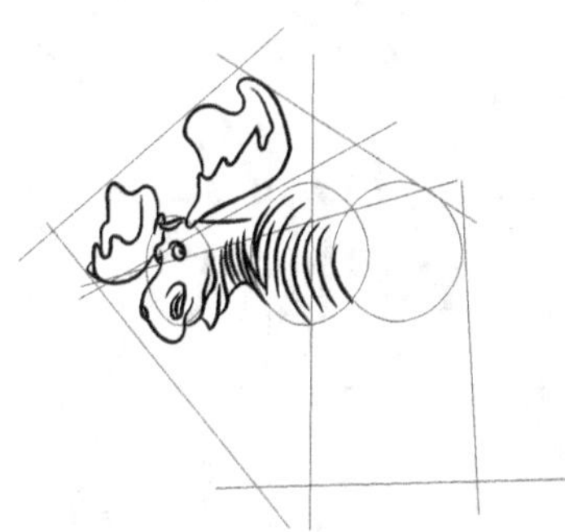

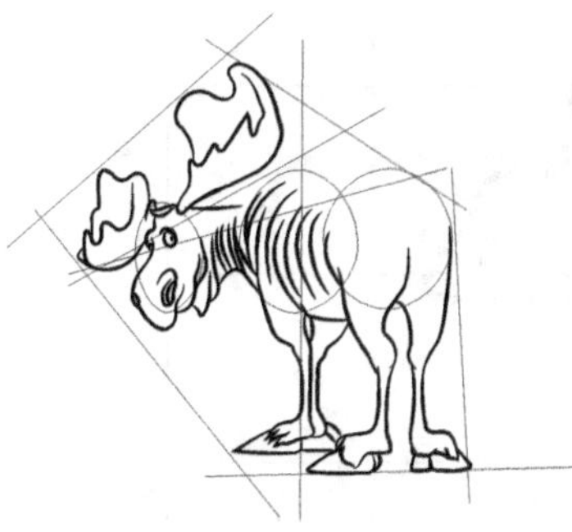
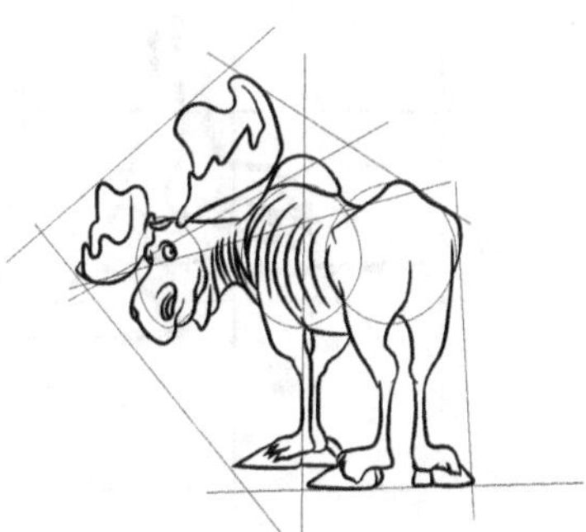
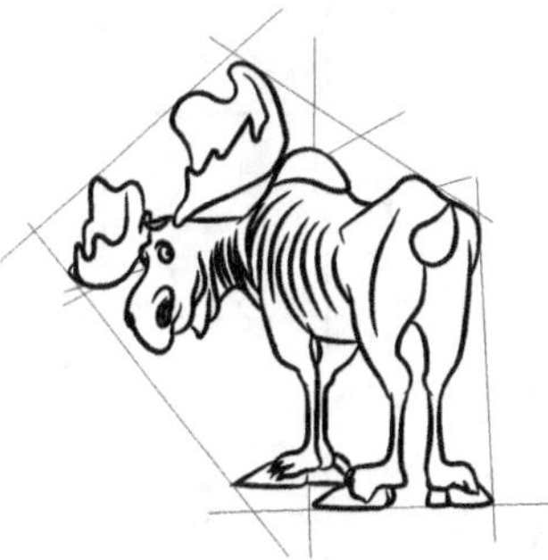

Moose are the largest members of the deer family, found in North America, Europe, and Asia. They have long legs, a distinctive dewlap called a "bell," and large, palmate antlers in males. Moose are solitary herbivores, primarily eating aquatic plants and shrubs. They are strong swimmers and can run up to 35 mph.

33. Animals with eyes to each side of their head are on the lookout for danger. Animals with eyes close together at the front of their head are on the lookout for prey.

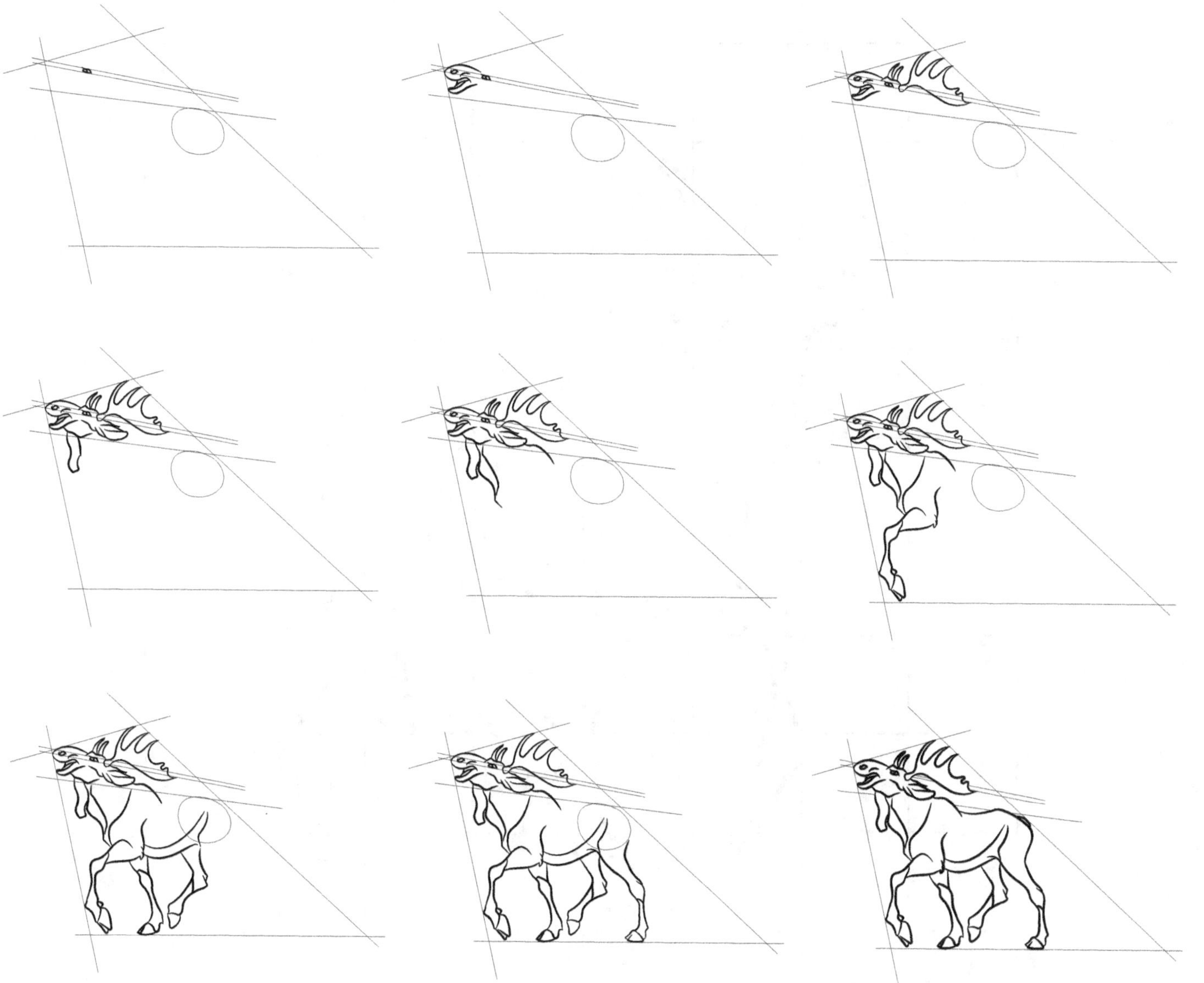

Reindeer, or caribou in North America, are large deer found in Arctic and Subarctic regions. Both males and females have antlers. They migrate long distances, have thick fur, and hooves adapted for snow. Reindeer are key to indigenous cultures and Christmas folklore.

34. Add extra details to your drawings to make more unique characters.

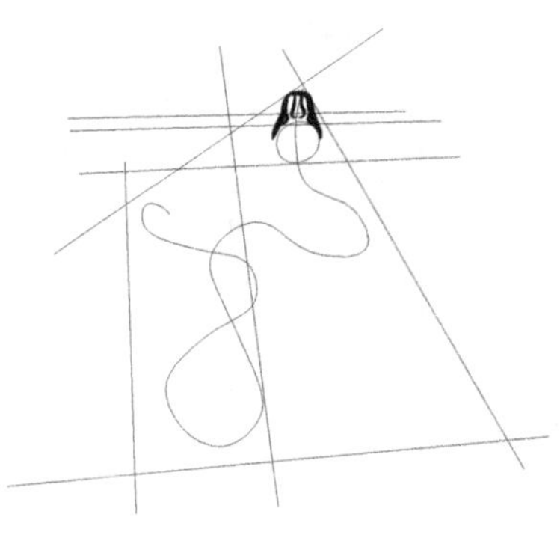
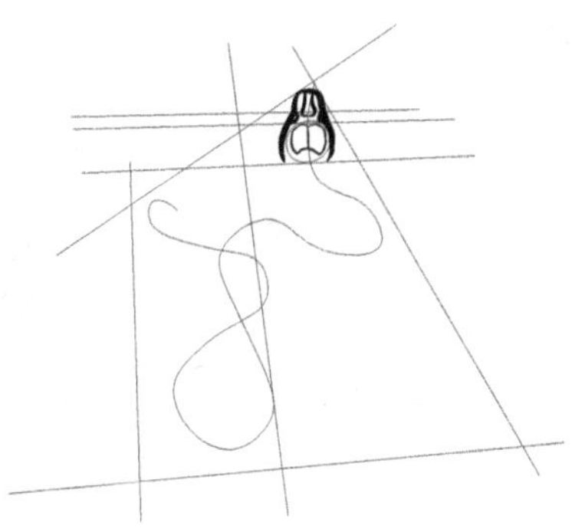
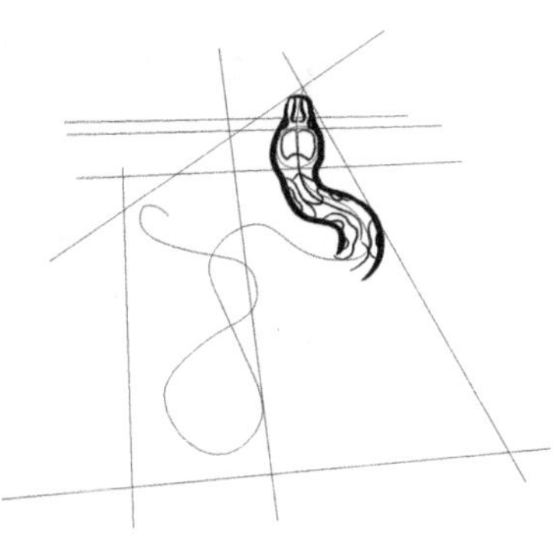

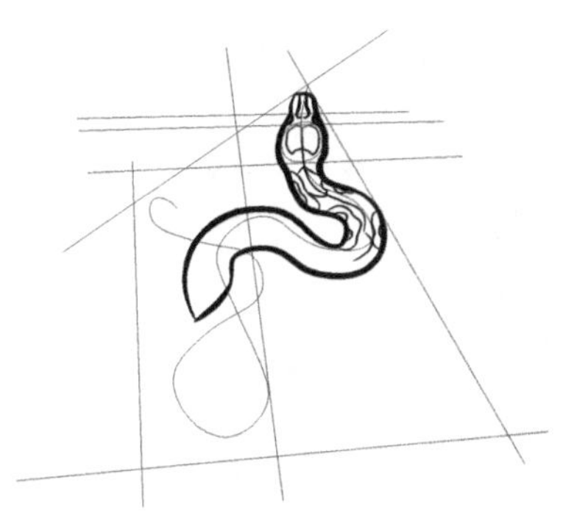
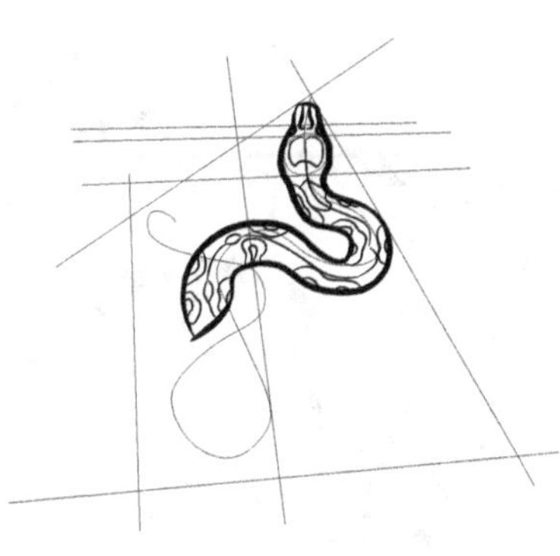
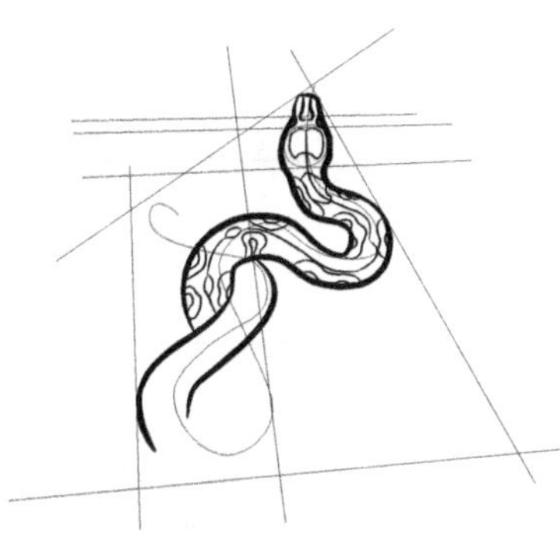

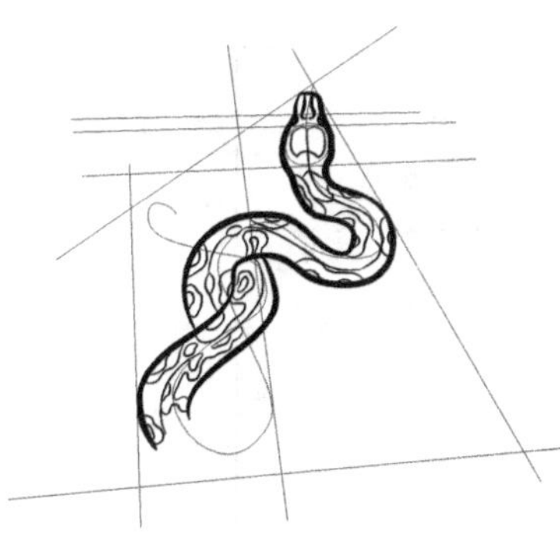
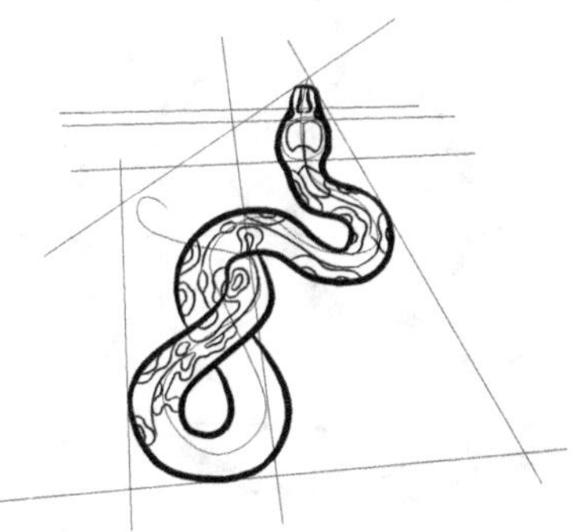

Pythons are large, non-venomous snakes found in Africa, Asia, and Australia. Known for their constricting method of subduing prey, they have heat-sensing pits for detecting warm-blooded animals. Pythons can grow very large, with some species exceeding 20 feet in length. They are popular in the pet trade and feature prominently in various cultures and myths.

35. It is very rare to see animals of the same breed that are exactly alike. It is usually small details that separate them.

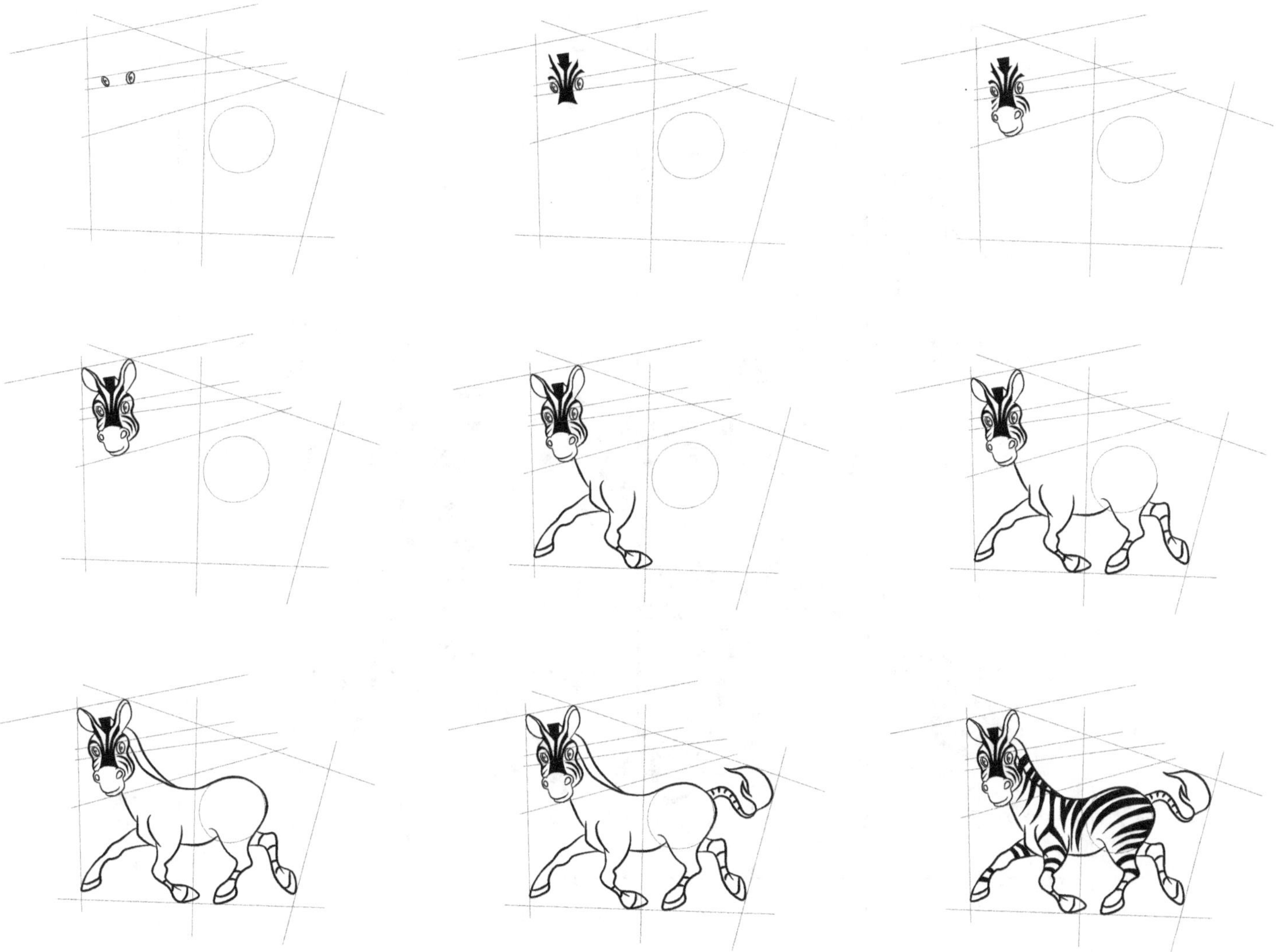

Zebras are iconic African mammals known for their black and white striped coats, which are unique to each individual. They are herbivores found in grasslands and savannas, living in social groups led by a dominant stallion. Zebras are fast runners and use their stripes for camouflage and group recognition.

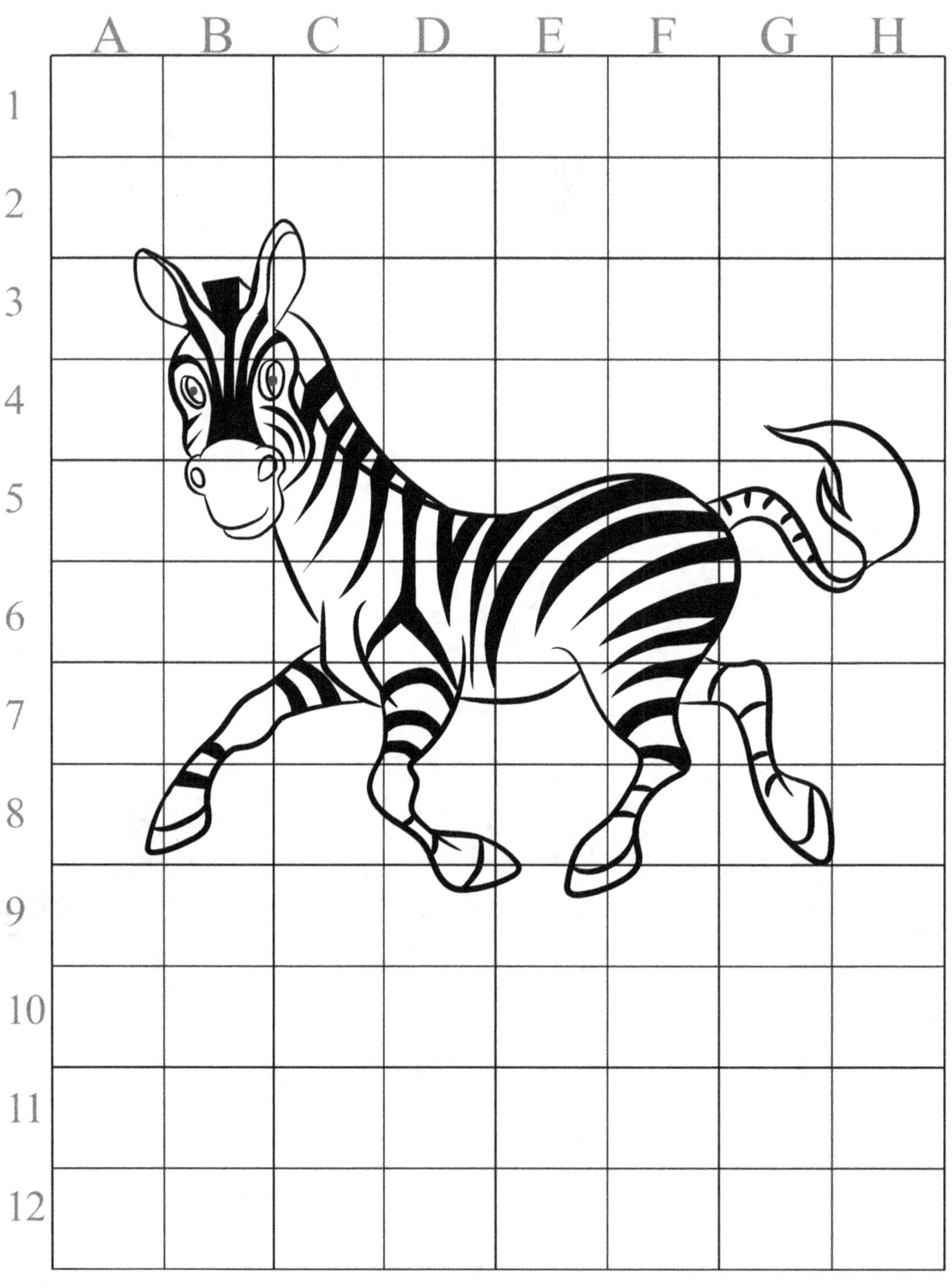

36. More complex characters require a lot more planning. One small step at time is the best approach to take, as all of those steps will add up.

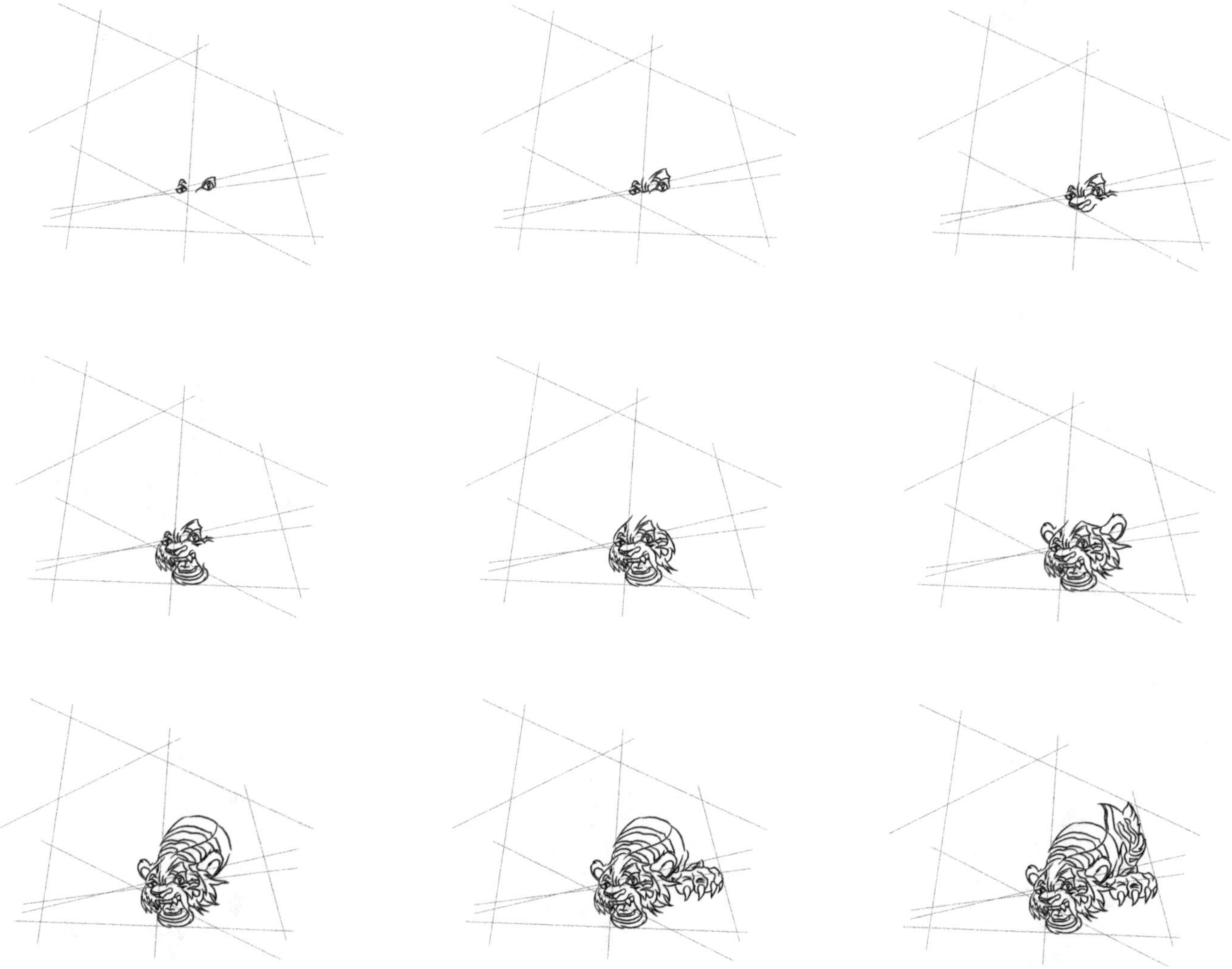

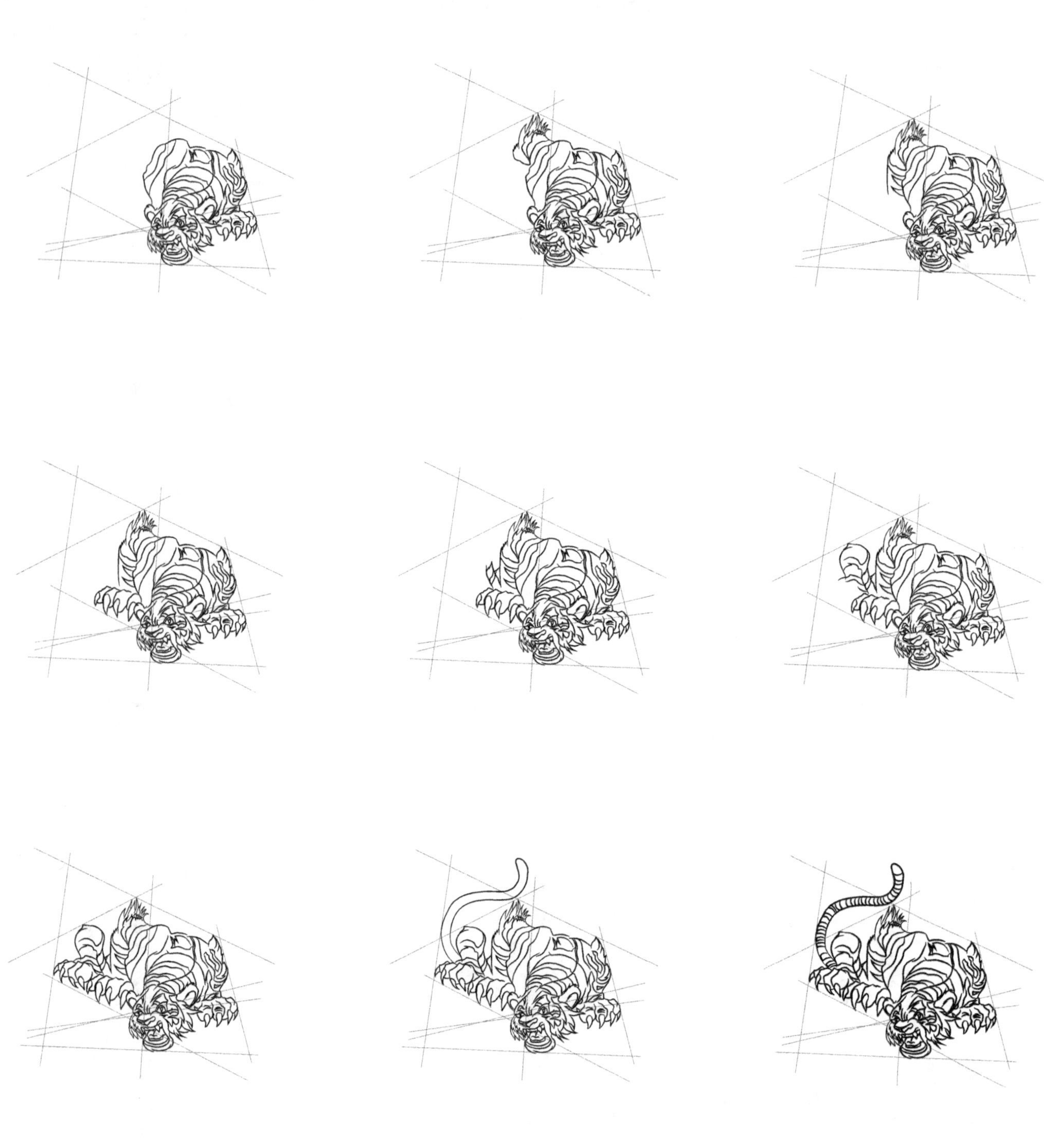

www.ingramcontent.com/pod-product-compliance
Lightning Source LLC
Chambersburg PA
CBHW081228130726
47997CB00009B/2811